MASTERPIECES OF PAINTING

from the

NATIONAL GALLERY OF ART

Edited by

HUNTINGTON CAIRNS

and

JOHN WALKER

NATIONAL GALLERY OF ART · WASHINGTON, D. C.

SMITHSONIAN INSTITUTION

RANDOM HOUSE · NEW YORK, N. Y.

Manufactured in the United States of America • *Produced by* THE BECK ENGRAVING COMPANY

PREFACE

This volume contains eighty-five reproductions in color of paintings from the collections of the National Gallery of Art, together with comments designed to assist the reader in an appreciation of them. There are also separate notes on the dates and provenance of each picture. In making the selection from the eight hundred paintings that now comprise the collections, the editors planned neither a presentation of the eighty-five greatest pictures in the Gallery's rich stores, nor a gleaning of their favorite works. They had two main objects in view. They intend the pictures to be representative of the variety and scope of the great National collection, and, at the same time, to illustrate the history of Western painting in each significant development from the thirteenth century to Cézanne. It is on that basis, for the most part, that some painters are represented by more than one picture, and other painters of equal stature are missing altogether. In the case of certain omissions among the American paintings, the editors must plead the gaps in this section of the Gallery's collection, a condition which is being corrected as rapidly as important examples can be obtained.

Opposite each picture the editors have placed a comment. These comments have been drawn from a variety of sources, novels, poetry, history, philosophy and formal writings on art. They are each about four hundred words in length, and have been chosen with an eye to their readability. These selections reveal many of the ideas that have been formulated in the effort to understand the meaning of painting; some are concerned with the subject of the particular work; others with the artist, his period or his philosophy; some are in verse, and a number are here published in English for the first time. Occasionally comments have been chosen because they seemed to summarize important aspects of the paintings, even though not referring directly to the pictures themselves. In the case of the quotation from T. S. Eliot, accompanying Raphael's Saint George and the Dragon, although this picture was not present to the poet's mind we believe that the excerpt nevertheless states in the words of poetry the mystical intention of the painting. We anticipate our critics in the realization that there are other selections that might have been made. There has been no purpose to present a general summary or even an outline of the factual history of Western art. Those facts are readily available in standard histories.

The notes that are placed after the comments give, within the limits of the space available, facts about the pictures which are of special interest to the serious student. However, in most instances they should also convey to the general reader a fuller understanding of the place of the picture in the history of painting.

The editors wish to acknowledge their special gratitude to Colonel Harry A. McBride, Administrator of the National Gallery of Art, for his indispensable contributions to the design and execution of this volume.

H. C.
J. W.

INTRODUCTION

By DAVID E. FINLEY
Director, National Gallery of Art

This book is intended to provide a representative view of the resources of the National Gallery of Art in the field of painting. Although the Gallery was not established until 1937, and did not open its doors to the public until 1941, those resources, as this volume reveals, are extensive. They cover Western painting from its origin in Byzantium to its development in the early part of the twentieth century in this country and Europe. Every school of importance is represented, and most of the world's outstanding painters. In both quality and range, the collection of the National Gallery is now one of the great collections of the world.

Supported by public appropriation, the National Gallery belongs to no one city or state but to all the people of the country. The Chairman of its Board of Trustees is the Chief Justice of the United States; the Board includes also the Secretary of State, the Secretary of the Treasury, and the Secretary of the Smithsonian Institution, representing the Government, and five distinguished private citizens representing the public.

For the people of the United States a national gallery of art serves many functions. It is charged with the particular responsibility of assembling a great national collection of paintings, sculpture and the graphic arts, representative, in each category, of the best in the artistic heritage of Europe and America. The value of that collection will be in proportion to the amount of pleasure it gives to those who view it. "We have not that respect for art that is one of the glories of France," the late Justice Holmes wrote in 1928, "but to many people the superfluous is the necessary, and it seems to me that government does not go beyond its sphere in attempting to make life livable for them."

Since he wrote we have seen in this country a marked transformation in taste, for which many factors have been responsible. Music has been brought within everyone's reach, by symphony orchestras in the larger cities and elsewhere by radio, so that people in all parts of the United States not only know good music but also demand the best in composition and performance. In the visual arts, the change in taste is due, first of all, to the growing interest in art fostered by the great museums in New York, Chicago and other cities, with their important collections and long tradition of public service. These resources have been supplemented by private collections which have been opened to the public, and by the other institutions comprising the 224 public art museums in the United States. Still another factor has been the establishment of the National Gallery, which has further focussed the Nation's attention on art. The astonishing attendance record at the National Gallery, which exceeds 2,000,000 visitors a year, is convincing evidence of the widespread interest in the fine arts which exists today on the part of the public.

In this country the National Gallery of Art has still another function as the Government agency charged with responsibility for sponsoring or carrying on many official activities in the field of art. Thus it has established, at the request of the Department of State, an Inter-American Office,

6

which will provide official sponsorship for Inter-American art projects and related activities. In this way the Gallery becomes the channel of communication in matters relating to art between this Government and the national galleries and Ministries of Fine Arts of the other American republics. Special government art exhibitions, such as the war paintings of the Armed Services, are held in the National Gallery of Art; and temporary art commissions, such as the President's Commission for the Protection and Salvage of Artistic and Historic Monuments in War Areas, have their headquarters in its building. At the request of the Departments of State and Treasury, the Gallery was made the custodian of the collection of art objects belonging to the French Government and various French museums and individuals, held in this country for safe-keeping during the Second World War. The Gallery was given the Index of American Design, which consists of 22,000 drawings and water colors, made under the auspices of the United States Government as a pictorial record of American source material in design and craftsmanship from early Colonial days to the close of the nineteenth century. The wealth of native craftsmanship and design thus preserved for future generations will eventually be published, and in that way, and by circulation of the original drawings among other museums, will be made available to artisans, manufacturers and others in the field of design and craftsmanship.

For the American artist the National Gallery has an important rôle. As Renoir said, "It is at the museum that one learns to paint." Renoir had the advantage of the Louvre, but in America, even a generation or two ago, artists such as Whistler and Mary Cassatt were obliged to go abroad to study the masterpieces of Europe. Today many of the greatest masterpieces are here, and an artist can find the sustenance he needs in the National Gallery in Washington and in other museums in all parts of the United States. He can also have the satisfaction of knowing that his work, if it meets the requirements of great art, may eventually find its rightful place in the Nation's collection in Washington.

"A museum is like a living organism — it requires continual and tender care. It must grow, or it will perish," a great student of museums, Sir William Flower, wrote many years ago. From the beginning the Gallery has enjoyed the utmost good fortune in the interest which American collectors have taken in its continued growth. The large, white marble building, with its severe classic lines, its porticos supported by Ionic columns, and its low dome, was the gift of the late Andrew W. Mellon. Begun in June 1937, it was completed in December 1940, and was erected under the direction of Paul Mellon, Donald D. Shepard and David K. E. Bruce, trustees of The A. W. Mellon Educational and Charitable Trust. Mr. Mellon and the Trust gave also a collection of paintings and sculpture, containing fine examples of the works of the greatest masters. In respect to quality, that collection has been made, by the Act of Congress establishing the Gallery, the norm or standard by which all gifts to the institution are measured. Mr. Mellon provided the Trust with a substantial sum of money, which was given to the Gallery and is used as the beginning of an Endowment Fund, for the purchase of works of art and for other purposes not connected with the upkeep of the building. As other donors increase the Endowment Fund, it will provide not only for further acquisitions but also for publications, fellowships, lectures, extension work, art research, concerts, loan exhibitions and other activities, which will extend the influence and usefulness of the National Gallery to all parts of this country and the world.

In making his gift, Mr. Mellon expressed the hope that the Gallery should become a joint enterprise on the part of the Government, on the one hand, and magnanimous citizens, on the other, who are interested in the arts and desire to contribute to their advancement. This hope was realized, even before the Gallery opened, by the action of Mr. Samuel H. Kress, who gave to the

Nation his large and important collection of paintings and sculpture. That collection is one of the few outside of Italy which gives a complete and systematic representation of the Italian School of painting, with fine examples of the greatest masters such as Duccio, Giotto, Piero della Francesca, Botticelli, Raphael, Bellini, Giorgione, Titian, Tintoretto and Tiepolo. In addition, the Kress Collection includes works of many of the greatest Italian and French sculptors, and an entire room of paintings by French eighteenth-century artists such as Watteau, Fragonard, Boucher and Drouais.

The late Joseph E. Widener also gave, during his lifetime, the famous collection formed by his father and himself — a collection notable not only for the variety and beauty of the works of art which it contains but for the faultless discrimination shown in the choice of each object. In the collection are more than a hundred paintings, including works by Raphael, Bellini, Titian, El Greco, Rembrandt, Vermeer, Van Dyck, Gainsborough, Turner, Constable, Manet, Renoir and Degas. There are also well-known pieces of sculpture by Italian and French artists, as well as ceramics, tapestries, and drawings.

A great gap in the Gallery's collection was filled when Mr. Chester Dale sent from his home in New York paintings which occupy several large rooms in the Gallery and provide a complete representation of nineteenth-century art in France, with particular emphasis on the works of the Impressionists and Post-Impressionists. In addition to paintings by David, Delacroix, Corot, Manet, Degas, Monet, Cézanne, Renoir, van Gogh and Toulouse-Lautrec, the collection includes outstanding examples of the work of Mary Cassatt, the distinguished American artist, who lived for many years in France and was closely identified there with the Impressionist School. Mr. Dale has also made an addition to the Gallery's collection of old masters by his gift of paintings by El Greco, Tintoretto, Rubens, Boucher, Chardin and others.

Another important accession was the gift by Mr. Lessing J. Rosenwald of over 8,000 prints and drawings, including many unique woodcuts and engravings by the pioneer print-makers of the fifteenth century, as well as superb impressions of virtually all the great masters of the graphic arts. The print room of the National Gallery has also been enriched by the gift of many fine prints from other donors.

Additional gifts of one or more important paintings or pieces of sculpture have been made by Dr. Horace Binney, Mrs. Ralph Harman Booth, Mr. and Mrs. George W. Davison, Mr. Frederic A. Delano, Mrs. Gordon Dexter, Mr. and Mrs. P. H. B. Frelinghuysen, the children of the late Right Reverend William Lawrence, Miss Ethelyn McKinney, the W. L. and May T. Mellon Foundation, Mrs. Robert Noyes, Mr. Duncan Phillips, Mr. Herbert L. Pratt, Mrs. John W. Simpson, Mrs. Jesse Isidor Straus, Mr. Clarence Van Dyke Tiers, Mrs. Felix Warburg, and the Harris Whittemore Collection.

Thus the National Gallery, with its growing collections and expanding activities, has already become a joint enterprise on the part of the government and generous-minded individuals, intent on giving America the best obtainable in the field of art. Already, too, it is fulfilling the hope, expressed at its dedication, that it would become not a static but a living institution, growing in usefulness and importance to artists, scholars and the general public. The future of the National Gallery can be measured only by the future of the country which it serves.

ACKNOWLEDGMENTS

The editors wish to thank the members of the staff of the National Gallery of Art who aided in the preparation of this volume, and particularly Mr. Stephen S. Pichetto for his valuable assistance. They also are indebted to Dr. Elio Gianturco, of The Library of Congress, and Mr. F. L. Teach, of Baltimore, Md., for special translations.

Acknowledgments are made to the following institutions for their cooperation in providing source material: Brooklyn Museum, New York City; Bryn Mawr College Library, Bryn Mawr, Pa.; Catholic University Library, Washington, D. C.; Dumbarton Oaks Research Library, Washington, D. C.; Enoch Pratt Free Library, Baltimore, Md.; Folger Shakespeare Library, Washington, D. C.; Georgetown University Library, Washington, D. C.; Girard College Library, Philadelphia, Pa.; The Grosvenor Library, Buffalo, N. Y.; Harvard College Library, Cambridge, Mass.; The Library of Congress, Washington, D. C.; National Collection of Fine Arts, Washington, D. C.; New York Public Library, New York City; Peabody Library, Baltimore, Md.; Philadelphia Museum of Art, Philadelphia, Pa.; Phillips Memorial Gallery, Washington, D. C.; Princeton University Library, Princeton, N. J.; Public Library of Washington, D. C.; Walters Art Gallery, Baltimore, Md.; Yale University Library, New Haven, Conn. The Samuel H. Kress Foundation also put its extensive research material at the disposal of the editors.

For permission to reprint selections in this volume the editors are indebted also as follows: from *Mont Saint Michel and Chartres*, by Henry Adams, copyright 1904, by permission of Houghton Mifflin Company; from *The Life of Reason*, by George Santayana, copyright 1905, by permission of Charles Scribner's Sons; from *The Italian Painters of the Renaissance*, by Bernhard Berenson, 1930, two selections by permission of the Clarendon Press, Oxford; from *Alesso Baldovinetti*, by Ruth Wedgwood Kennedy, copyright 1938, two selections by permission of Yale University Press; from *The Golden Legend* of Jacobus de Voragine, copyright 1941, by permission of Longmans, Green and Co.; from *Vision and Design*, by Roger Fry, 1920, two selections by courtesy of Coward McCann, Inc.; from *The Notebooks of Leonardo da Vinci*, 1939, by permission of Reynal and Hitchcock; from *Along the Road*, by Aldous Huxley, copyright 1925, two selections by permission of Harper & Brothers; from *History of Italian Literature*, by Francesco De Sanctis, copyright 1931, by permission of Harcourt, Brace & Co.; from *Four Quartets*, by T. S. Eliot, copyright 1943, by permission of Harcourt, Brace & Co.; from *Italian Hours*, by Henry James, copyright 1909, by permission of Houghton Mifflin Company; from *Don Fernando*, by W. Somerset Maugham, copyright 1935, reprinted by permission of Doubleday, Doran and Co., Inc.; from *The Soul of Spain*, by Havelock Ellis, copyright 1908, by permission of Houghton Mifflin Company; from *The Masters of Past Time* by Eugène Fromentin, 1913, by permission of E. P. Dutton & Co.; from *The Life of Forms in Art*, by Henri Focillon, copyright 1934, by permission of Yale University Press; from *Promenades of an Impressionist*, by James Huneker, copyright 1910, by permission of Charles Scribner's Sons; from *Christmas Holiday*, by W. Somerset Maugham, copyrighted 1939, by permission of Doubleday, Doran and Co.; from *A Study of History*, by Arnold J. Toynbee, 1934, by permission of the Clarendon Press, Oxford; from *The Aristocratic Journey; Being the Letters of Mrs. Basil Hall*, edited by Una Pope-Hennessy, copyright 1931, by courtesy of G. P. Putnam's Sons; from *Studies in Seven Arts*, by Arthur Symons, copyright 1906, by permission of E. P. Dutton & Co.; from *Pots and Pans*, by Arthur Edwin Bye, copyright 1921, by permission of Princeton University Press; from *Renoir, An Intimate Record*, by Ambroise Vollard, copyright 1925, by permission of Alfred A. Knopf; from *A Room of One's Own*, by Virginia Woolf, copyright 1929, by permission of Harcourt, Brace and Co.; from *"Remington and Winslow Homer,"* by John Wheelwright, *Hound & Horn*, 1933, by permission of Lincoln Kirstein; from *The Paintings of D. H. Lawrence*, 1929, by permission of Mrs. Frieda Lawrence.

For some selections the editors have made use of translations already available, as follows: Boccaccio, *The Decameron*, translated by W. K. Kelly; Dante, *The Divine Comedy (Paradiso)*, translated by Philip Henry Wicksteed; Vasari, *Lives*, translated by Gaston du C. de Vere; Jacobus de Voragine, *The Golden Legend*, translated and adapted by Granger Ryan and Helmut Ripperger; Leonardo da Vinci, *Notebooks*, arranged and translated by Edward MacCurdy; De Sanctis, *History of Italian Literature*, translated by Joan Redfern; Castiglione, *The Courtier*, translated by A. P. Castiglione; Machiavelli, *The Art of War*, anonymous translation; Ovid, *Fasti*, translated by Henry T. Riley; Francisco de Hollanda, *Four Dialogues on Painting*, translated by Aubrey F. G. Bell; Hegel, *The Philosophy of Fine Art*, translated by F. P. B. Osmaston; Huizinga, *The Waning of the Middle Ages*, translated by F. Hopman; de Piles, *The Principles of Painting*, anonymous translation; Fromentin, *The Masters of Past Time*, anonymous translation; Focillon, *The Life of Forms in Art*, translated by C. Beecher Hogan and George Kubler; Sainte-Beuve, *Causeries du lundi*, translated by E. J. Trechmann; Spengler, *The Decline of the West*, excerpt translated by Arnold J. Toynbee (*A Study of History*, vol. 3, 1934); Vollard, *Renoir, An Intimate Record*, translated by Harold L. Van Doren and Randolph T. Weaver; van Gogh, *Further Letters of Vincent van Gogh*, anonymous translation.

We also wish to credit other sources as follows: *"Fine Arts,"* by William Hazlitt, from *The Encyclopaedia Britannica*, 1817; letter to Gaspero Ballini, from *L'Aretino*, by Lodovico Dolce, 1910; Lectures on Landscape Painting, by John Constable, from *Memoirs of the Life of John Constable*, by C. R. Leslie, 1845; the "Discourses," from the *Collected Works* of Sir Joshua Reynolds, 1798; quotation, Henry Sargent, from *History of the Rise and Progress of the Arts of Design in the United States*, by William Dunlap, 1834; letter of Captain George Mercer, from *George Washington as an Inventor and Promoter of the Useful Arts*, by J. M. Toner, 1892; letter of a Virginia woman, from *George Washington*, by Paul Leicester Ford, 1896; letter of Mrs. Basil Hall, from *The Aristocratic Journey*, edited by Una Pope-Hennessy, 1931; "Various Subjects of Landscape," by John Constable, from *The Published Mezzotints of David Lucas after John Constable*, by Andrew Shirley, 1930; letter to Miss Erskine, from *Memoir and Letters of Sara Coleridge*, edited by Edith Coleridge, 1874; "Exhibition of Paintings in Fresco," from *A Bibliography of William Blake*, by Geoffrey Keynes, 1921; "Edouard Manet," from *Mes Haines*, by Emile Zola, 1879. For additional data on Winslow Homer the editors are indebted to Mr. Lloyd Goodrich.

CONTENTS

MASTERPIECES OF PAINTING

BYZANTINE SCHOOL · XIII Century

Enthroned Madonna and Child

You can start at Byzantium with the Empress Helena in 326, or with the Council of Ephesus in 431. You will find the Virgin acting as the patron saint of Constantinople and of the imperial residence, under as many names as Artemis or Aphrodite had borne. As God-mother (Θεομητηρ), Deipara (Θεοτοκος), Path-finder (Ὁδηγητρια), she was the chief favorite of the eastern empire, and her picture was carried at the head of every procession and hung on the wall of every hut and hovel, as it is still wherever the Greek Church goes. In the year 610, when Heraclius sailed from Carthage to dethrone Phocas at Constantinople, his ships carried the image of the Virgin at their mast-heads. In 1143, just before the *flèche* on the Chartres *clocher* was begun, the Basileus John Comnenus died, and so devoted was he to the Virgin that, on a triumphal entry into Constantinople, he put the image of the Mother of God in his chariot, while he himself walked. In the western Church the Virgin had always been highly honored, but it was not until the crusades that she began to overshadow the Trinity itself. Then her miracles became more frequent and her shrines more frequented, so that Chartres, soon after 1100, was rich enough to build its western Portal with Byzantine splendor. . . .

The Church had crowned and enthroned her almost from the beginning, and could not have dethroned her if it would. In all Christian art,—sculpture or mosaic, painting or poetry,—the Virgin's rank was expressly asserted. Saint Bernard like John Comnenus, and probably at the same time (1120-1140) chanted hymns to the Virgin as Queen:

O salutaris Virgo Stella Maris
Generans prolem, Aequitatis solem,
Lucis auctorem, Retinens pudorem,
　　Suscipe laudem!

Coeli Regina Per quam medicina
Datur aegrotis, Gratia devotis,
Gaudium moestis, Mundo lux cœlestis,
　　Spesque salutis;

Aula regalis, Virgo specialis,
Posce medelam Nobis et tutelam,
Suscipe vota, Precibusque cuncta
　　Pelle molesta!

O savior Virgin, Star of Sea,
Who bore for child the Sun of Justice,
The source of Light, Virgin always
　　Hear our praise!

Queen of Heaven who have given
Medicine to the sick, Grace to the devout,
Joy to the sad, heaven's light to the world
　　And hope of salvation;

Court royal, Virgin typical,
Grant us cure and guard,
Accept our vows, and by prayers
　　Drive all griefs away!

Henry Adams
Mont Saint Michel and Chartres (1904)

Wood. Height 33 in.; width 21 in. (0.84 x 0.53). Thirteenth century. Berenson believes this panel to have been painted in Constantinople around the year 1200 (*Dedalo*, 1921). It was discovered about 1920 in a Spanish convent, which also possessed a similar Madonna now in the Collection of Mrs. Otto H. Kahn, New York. Both Madonnas may have been brought to Spain by some crusading knight or ecclesiastic returned from a pilgrimage to the East. Collections: A convent in Calahorra, Aragon, Spain. *Mellon Collection*, 1937.

DUCCIO DI BUONINSEGNA · SIENESE c. 1255-1319

The Calling of the Apostles Peter and Andrew

The whole history of painting may be strung on this single thread — the effort to reconstitute impressions, first the dramatic impression and then the sensuous. A summary and symbolic representation of things is all that at first is demanded; the point is to describe something pictorially and recall people's names and actions. It is characteristic of archaic painting to be quite discursive and symbolic; each figure is treated separately and stuck side by side with the others upon a golden ground. The painter is here smothered in the recorder, in the annalist; only those perceptions are allowed to stand which have individual names or chronicle facts mentioned in the story. But vision is really more sensuous and rich than report, if art is only able to hold vision in suspense and make it explicit. When painting is still at this stage, and is employed on hieroglyphics, it may reach the maximum of decorative splendour. Whatever sensuous glow finer representations may later acquire will be not sensuous merely, but poetical.

     ·   ·   ·   ·

Illustration has nevertheless an intellectual function by which it diverges altogether from decoration and even, in the narrowest sense of the word, from art: for the essence of illustration lies neither in use nor in beauty. The illustrator's impulse is to reproduce and describe given objects. He wishes in the first place to force observers — overlooking all logical scruples — to call his work by the name of its subject matter; and then he wishes to inform them further, through his representation, and to teach them to apprehend the real object as, in its natural existence, it might never have been apprehended. His first task is to translate the object faithfully into his special medium; his second task, somewhat more ambitious, is so to penetrate into the object during that process of translation that this translation may become at the same time analytic and imaginative, in that it signalises the object's structure and emphasises its ideal suggestions. In such reproduction both hand and mind are called upon to construct and build up a new apparition; but here construction has ceased to be chiefly decorative or absolute in order to become representative. The æsthetic element in art has begun to recede before the intellectual; and sensuous effects, while of course retained and still studied, seem to be impressed into the service of ideas.

GEORGE SANTAYANA
The Life of Reason (1905)

Wood. Height 16¾ in.; width 17¾ in. (0.43 x 0.45). The Byzantine tradition of painting culminated in the Maestà, or Virgin in Majesty, executed by Duccio for the Cathedral of Siena between 1308 and 1311. This great double altarpiece was later removed from the cathedral, dismembered, and placed in the Opera del Duomo. All but eight of the ninety-two panels which originally covered the front and back of the altarpiece still remain in Siena. The present picture formed part of the predella which faced the east end of the church. A second panel from the Maestà, the Nativity with the Prophets Isaiah and Ezekiel, is also in the National Gallery of Art. Collections: The Cathedral of Siena; Robert H. and Evelyn Benson, London; Clarence H. Mackay, Roslyn, New York. *Kress Collection*, 1939.

GIOTTO · Florentine c. 1266-1336

Madonna and Child

As it often happens that fortune hides, under the meanest trades in life, the greatest virtues, which has been proved by Pampinea, so are the greatest geniuses found frequently lodged by nature in the most deformed and misshapen bodies. This truth was verified in two of our own citizens, as I am now going to relate. For the one, who was called Forese da Rabatta, being a little deformed mortal, with a flat Dutch face, worse than any of the family of the Baronci, was yet esteemed by most men a repository of the civil law. And the other, whose name was Giotto, had such a prodigious fancy, that there was nothing in Nature, the parent of all things, but he could imitate it with his pencil so well, and draw it so like, as to deceive our very senses, making them imagine that to be the very thing itself which was only his painting; therefore, having brought that art again to light, which had lain buried for many ages, under the errors of such as aimed more to captivate the eyes of the ignorant, than to please the understandings of those who were really judges, he may deservedly be called one of the lights and glories of our city, and the rather as being master of his art, notwithstanding his modesty would never suffer himself to be so esteemed. . . . But though his excellence in his profession was so wonderful, yet as to his person and aspect he had no way the advantage of Signor Forese. . . .

These two worthies had each his country seat at Mugello, and Forese being gone thither in the vacation time, and riding upon an unsightly steed, chanced to meet there with Giotto, who was no better equipped than himself, and they returned together to Florence. Travelling slowly along, as they were able to go no faster, they were overtaken by a great shower of rain, and forced to take shelter in a poor man's house, who was well known to them both; and as there was no appearance of the weather's clearing up, and each was desirous of getting home that night, they borrowed two old russet cloaks, and two rusty hats, and proceeded on their journey. After they had got a good part of their way, thoroughly wet, and covered with dirt and mire, which their two shuffling steeds had thrown upon them, and which by no means improved their looks, it began to clear up at last, and they, who had hitherto said but little to each other, now turned to discourse together. Forese, as he jogged on, listening to Giotto, who was excellent at telling a story, began at last to view him attentively from head to foot, and seeing him in that wretched dirty pickle, without ever thinking of his own plight, he fell a laughing, and said, "Do you suppose, Giotto, if a stranger were to meet with you now, who had never seen you before, that he would imagine you to be the best painter in the world, as you really are?" Giotto readily replied, "Yes, sir, I believe he might think so, if looking at you at the same time, he could ever conclude that you had learned your A, B, C." At this Forese was sensible of his mistake, finding himself well paid in his own coin.

Giovanni Boccaccio
Il Decamerone (1353)

Wood. Height 34⅝ in.; width 25 in. (0.88 x 0.64). Painted c. 1320. It is believed that this painting was once the central panel of an altarpiece to which the Saint Stephen of the Horne Foundation, Florence, originally belonged. Longhi has also suggested (*Dedalo,* 1930) that the two panels in the André Collection (Châalis), representing Saint John the Evangelist and Saint Lawrence, were formerly part of the same polyptych, and he believes that this was the altarpiece mentioned by Ghiberti and Vasari as having been painted by Giotto for the Badia, Florence. Collections: Edouard de Max, Paris; Henry Goldman, New York. *Kress Collection,* 1939.

MASACCIO · FLORENTINE 1401-1427/28

Profile Portrait of a Young Man

Giotto born again, starting where death had cut short his advance, instantly making his own all that had been gained during his absence, and profiting by the new conditions, the new demands — imagine such an avatar, and you will understand Masaccio.

Giotto we know already, but what were the new conditions, the new demands? The medieval skies had been torn asunder and a new heaven and a new earth had appeared, which the abler spirits were already inhabiting and enjoying. Here new interests and new values prevailed. The thing of sovereign price was the power to subdue and to create; of sovereign interest all that helped man to know the world he was living in and his power over it. To the artist the change offered a field of the freest activity. It is always his business to reveal to an age its ideals. But what room was there for sculpture and painting — arts whose first purpose it is to make us realize the material significance of things — in a period like the Middle Ages, when the human body was denied all intrinsic significance? In such an age the figure artist can thrive, as Giotto did, only in spite of it, and as an isolated phenomenon. In the Renaissance, on the contrary, the figure artist had a demand made on him such as had not been made since the great Greek days, to reveal to a generation believing in man's power to subdue and to possess the world, the physical types best fitted for the task. . . .

Types, in themselves of the manliest, he presents with a sense for the materially significant which makes us realize to the utmost their power and dignity; and the spiritual significance thus gained he uses to give the highest import to the event he is portraying; this import, in turn, gives a higher value to the types, and thus, whether we devote our attention to his types or to his action, Masaccio keeps us on a high plane of reality and significance. In later painting we shall easily find greater science, greater craft, and greater perfection of detail, but greater reality, greater significance, I venture to say, never. Dust-bitten and ruined though his Brancacci Chapel frescoes now are, I never see them without the strongest stimulation of my tactile consciousness. I feel that I could touch every figure, that it would yield a definite resistance to my touch, that I should have to expend thus much effort to displace it, that I could walk around it. In short, I scarcely could realize it more, and in real life I should scarcely realize it so well, the attention of each of us being too apt to concentrate itself upon some dynamic quality, before we have at all begun to realize the full material significance of the person before us. . . .

Masaccio, then, like Giotto a century earlier — himself the Giotto of an artistically more propitious world — was, as an artist, a great master of the significant, and, as a painter, endowed to the highest degree with a sense of tactile values, and with a skill in rendering them. In a career of but few years he gave to Florentine painting the direction it pursued to the end. In many ways he reminds us of the young Bellini. Who knows? Had he but lived as long, he might have laid the foundation for a painting not less delightful and far more profound than that of Venice.

BERNHARD BERENSON
The Italian Painters of the Renaissance (1930)

Wood. Height 16¾ in.; width 12¾ in. (0.43 x 0.32). Painted c. 1425. The present painting has been incorrectly grouped by some critics with the Olivieri portraits, which have been ascribed to Domenico Veneziano and Paolo Uccello. The attribution to Masaccio, on the convincing evidence of style, was first published in the 1843 catalogue of the Artaud de Montor Collection, and is supported by Berenson. One other portrait on panel, Profile of a Young Man, in the Isabella Gardner Museum, Boston, has been ascribed to Masaccio's own hand. Collections: Artaud de Montor, Paris. *Mellon Collection*, 1937.

FRA ANGELICO · FLORENTINE 1387-1455

The Madonna of Humility

Hilda's despondency, nevertheless, while it dulled her perceptions in one respect, had deepened them in another; she saw beauty less vividly, but felt truth, or the lack of it, more profoundly. She began to suspect that some, at least, of her venerated painters, had left an inevitable hollowness in their works, because, in the most renowned of them, they essayed to express to the world what they had not in their own souls. They deified their light and wandering affections, and were continually playing off the tremendous jest, alluded to above, of offering the features of some venal beauty to be enshrined in the holiest places. A deficiency of earnestness and absolute truth is generally discoverable in Italian pictures, after the art had become consummate. When you demand what is deepest, these painters have not wherewithal to respond. They substituted a keen intellectual perception, and a marvellous knack of external arrangement, instead of the live sympathy and sentiment which should have been their inspiration. And hence it happens, that shallow and worldly men are among the best critics of their works; a taste for pictorial art is often no more than a polish upon the hard enamel of an artificial character. Hilda had lavished her whole heart upon it, and found (just as if she had lavished it upon a human idol) that the greater part was thrown away.

For some of the earlier painters, however, she still retained much of her former reverence. Fra Angelico, she felt, must have breathed a humble aspiration between every two touches of his brush, in order to have made the finished picture such a visible prayer as we behold it, in the guise of a prim angel, or a saint without the human nature. Through all these dusky centuries, his works may still help a struggling heart to pray.

NATHANIEL HAWTHORNE
The Marble Faun (1860)

Wood. Height 24½ in.; width 18½ in. (0.62 x 0.47). Painted c. 1430-1440. The title, Madonna of Humility, is applied to representations of the Virgin in which she is shown seated on the ground. The symbolism of the Madonna of Humility is connected with Luke I, 48, "For he hath regarded the low estate of his handmaiden." This type of devotional picture, according to Meiss (*The Art Bulletin,* 1936), originated in Siena and was especially popular with the Dominicans and the Franciscans. Collections: Edward Steinkopff, London; Lady Seaforth, Canon Bridge, Scotland. *Mellon Collection,* 1937.

DOMENICO VENEZIANO · Florentine c. 1400-1461

Saint John in the Desert

Domenico's place in the fabric of Florentine painting is only beginning to be understood. Only in recent years has the list of his paintings lengthened from four to thirteen, and we are still in ignorance of the simplest facts about his life. But even a brief survey of his work will give us the figure of a painter whose intrinsic merit and historical significance cannot be overlooked. . . .

Domenico was not the first Italian to look at the out-of-door world around him. Petrarch and Boccaccio had praised the spring, and gardens had become a necessary luxury to the rich *signori* to relieve the sombre austerity of their dark-eaved palaces and crenellated farms. And as the world of nature grew in importance in men's lives, it became a proper subject for painting also. Masaccio drew stark branches on bare mountain sides behind his stern followers of Christ; Masolino painted the snowy mountains he passed through between Hungary and the Lombard plain; Angelico filled his background with gentle hills and convent gardens. But Domenico, more than they, had the real landscape sense, so common north of the Alps and so often denied to Italians, and his Lago di Garda, his La Verna, and his sunny rose garden in Nazareth, have more conviction of their own intrinsic worth. . . .

Vasari's picture of the care-free serenader, graceful and urbane, is not the man which the paintings reveal. The thousands of tiny strokes gradually working out a silken fold which in its luminosity almost foretells the brilliant cape of Velasquez's Pope, the multiplicity of planes in the face of St. John, the minute touches of a brush just wet enough so that every one suggests a leaf dazzling in the sunshine, the measured shadows from the incised cornices, all show how deeply Domenico had studied his technique, what patience and care he lavished on his work. To us, who know Fra Filippo perhaps better than his rival, Domenico's estimate of five years of constant work before the Barbadori altarpiece could be finished, seems a ridiculous exaggeration, but if we consider the methods which he used himself it seems more reasonable. The St. Lucy altarpiece might almost have taken five years! . . . . Even Baldovinetti, whose long line of ancestors belonged to the class which in Florence constituted its nobility in all but name, lacked that essential elegance, that refinement so aloof, so withdrawn into itself that it looks on the world through half-veiled eyes of quiet melancholy. Domenico Veneziano was an innovator but not a shattering genius. He painted little and much of that is lost. He was admired, perhaps, in his time, though never quite for what he was, and soon forgotten in the shadow of his more forceful or more prolific contemporaries.

RUTH WEDGWOOD KENNEDY
Alesso Baldovinetti (1938)

Wood. Height 11 in.; width 12¼ in. (0.28 x 0.32). Painted c. 1450. This panel belongs to the predella of the Saint Lucy altarpiece which was originally in Santa Lucia dei Magnoli, Florence, and which is now in the Uffizi, Florence. The predella was composed of the following five paintings arranged from left to right: Saint Francis Receiving the Stigmata and the painting reproduced on the right, both in the Kress Collection, National Gallery of Art; the Annunciation and the Miracle of Saint Zenobius, both in the Fitzwilliam Museum, Cambridge, England; and the Martyrdom of Saint Lucy in the Kaiser Friedrich Museum, Berlin. In the present painting the figure of Saint John was probably inspired by some classical statue. Collections: Santa Lucia dei Magnoli, Florence; Bernhard Berenson, Florence; Carl W. Hamilton, New York. *Kress Collection, 1939.*

GENTILE DA FABRIANO · UMBRIAN c. 1360-1427

Madonna and Child

Vergine madre, figlia del tuo figlio,
  umile ed alta più che creatura,
  termine fisso d' eterno consiglio,

tu se' colei, che l' umana natura
  nobilitasti sì che il suo Fattore
  non disdegnò di farsi sua fattura.

Nel ventre tuo si raccese l' amore,
  per lo cui caldo nell' eterna pace
  così è germinato questo fiore.

Qui sei a noi meridiana face
  di caritate, e giuso, intra i mortali,
  sei di speranza fontana vivace.

Donna, sei tanto grande e tanto vali,
  che qual vuol grazia ed a te non ricorre,
  sua disianza vuol volar senz' ali.

La tua benignità non pur soccorre
  a chi domanda, ma molte fiate
  liberamente al domandar precorre.

In te misericordia, in te pietate,
  in te magnificenza, in te s' aduna
  quantunque in creatura è di bontate.

Or questi, che dall' infima lacuna
  dell' universo infin qui ha vedute
  le vite spiritali ad una ad una,

supplica a te, per grazia, di virtute
  tanto che possa con gli occhi levarsi
  più alto verso l' ultima salute;

ed io, che mai per mio veder non arsi
  più ch' io fo per lo suo, tutti i miei preghi
  ti porgo, e prego che non sieno scarsi,

perchè tu ogni nube gli disleghi
  di sua mortalità coi preghi tuoi,
  sì che il sommo piacer gli si dispieghi.

Ancor ti prego, Regina che puoi
  ciò che tu vuoli, che conservi sani,
  dopo tanto veder, gli affetti suoi.

Vinca tua guardia i movimenti umani;
  vedi Beatrice con quanti beati
  per li miei preghi ti chiudon le mani.

Virgin mother, daughter of thy son, lowly
  and uplifted more than any creature,
  fixed goal of the eternal counsel,

thou art she who didst human nature so
  ennoble that its own Maker scorned
  not to become its making.

In thy womb was lit again the love under
  whose warmth in the eternal peace
  this flower hath thus unfolded.

Here art thou unto us the meridian
  torch of love, and there below with
  mortals art a living spring of hope.

Lady, thou art so great and hast such worth,
  that if there be who would have grace yet
  betaketh not himself to thee, his longing
  seeketh to fly without wings.

Thy kindliness not only succoureth whoso
  requesteth, but doth oftentimes freely
  forerun request.

In thee is tenderness, in thee is pity, in
  thee munificence, in thee united whatever
  in created being is of excellence.

Now he who from the deepest pool of the universe even to here hath seen the spirit-
  lives, one by one,

imploreth thee, of grace, for so much
  power as to be able to uplift his eyes
  more high towards final bliss;

and I, who never burned for my own vision
  more than I do for his, proffer thee all
  my prayers, and pray they be not scant,

that thou do scatter for him every cloud of
  his mortality with prayers of thine, so
  that the joy supreme may be unfolded to him.

And further do I pray thee, Queen who canst do
  all that thou wilt, that thou keep sound
  for him, after so great a vision, his affections.

Let thy protection vanquish human ferments;
  see Beatrice, with how many Saints, for
  my prayers folding hands.

DANTE ALIGHIERI
La Divina Commedia (c. 1305-c. 1320)

Wood. Height 37¾ in.; width 22¼ in. (0.96 x 0.57). Painted c. 1420. This panel is thought to have been painted just before Gentile's Adoration of the Magi, dated 1423 and now in the Uffizi, Florence. It is generally recognized as the most important example of his transitional style. Collections: Madame E. J. Sartoris, Paris; Alexander Barker, London; Henry Goldman, New York. *Kress Collection*, 1939.

FRA FILIPPO LIPPI · Florentine c. 1406-1469

The Annunciation

There was then in the Carmine a chapel that had been newly painted by Masaccio, which, being very beautiful, pleased Fra Filippo so greatly that he would haunt it every day for his recreation; and continually practising there in company with many young men, who were ever drawing in it, he surpassed the others by a great measure in dexterity and knowledge, insomuch that it was held certain that in time he would do something marvellous. Nay, not merely in his maturity, but even in his early childhood, he executed so many works worthy of praise that it was a miracle. . . .

Having been commissioned by the Nuns of S. Margherita to paint the panel of their high-altar, he was working at this when there came before his eyes a daughter of Francesco Buti, a citizen of Florence, who was living there as a ward or as a novice. Having set eyes on Lucrezia (for this was the name of the girl), who was very beautiful and graceful, Fra Filippo contrived to persuade the nuns to allow him to make a portrait of her for a figure of Our Lady in the work that he was doing for them. With this opportunity . . . . he stole her away from the nuns and took her off. . . . Whereupon the nuns were greatly disgraced by such an event, and her father, Francesco, who never smiled again, made every effort to recover her; but she, either through fear or for some other reason, refused to come back — nay, she insisted on staying with Filippo, to whom she bore a male child, who was also called Filippo, and who became, like his father, a very excellent and famous painter.

Giorgio Vasari
Le Vite de' piv eccellenti pittori, scvltori, e architettori (1568)

The most marvelous thing about him was that he so thoroughly assimilated the style of Masaccio that, after his death, people used to say in jest that the spirit of Masaccio had entered into the body of Fra Filippo. . . . This artist was most exceptional for his time in the accuracy of his drawing and the charm which he always strove to impart to his figures, in the beautiful expression of his heads, the variety and nobility of his drapery, and in a certain perfection and grandeur of style which is always evident, especially in the great works which he executed in fresco in the city of Prato and elsewhere, but also in his smaller pictures. These works show most remarkable judgment and that singular care which he constantly devoted to the expression, not only of actions but also of emotions. These are qualities not found in ordinary artists but only in those who have become superior to art itself through long study and wide experience in their craft.

Filippo Baldinucci
Notizie de' professori del disegno (1728)

Wood. Height 40½ in.; width 64 in. (1.03 x 1.63). Painted 1445-1450. Vasari states that Filippo Lippi painted for the Palazzo Vecchio "an Annunciation on a panel, which is over a door; and over another door in the said Palace he also painted a Saint Bernard." Albertini (*Memoriale*, 1510), says that one panel was painted for the Main Chancery and the other for the Old Chancery of the palace. It is probable that the large Annunciation reproduced on the right-hand page, which is suitable in size and shape for an overdoor, is that mentioned by Vasari and Albertini as executed for the Palazzo Vecchio. Collections: Palazzo Vecchio, Florence (?); Percy Straus, New York. *Kress Collection*, 1939.

ALESSO BALDOVINETTI · FLORENTINE c. 1425-1499

The Annunciation

A mixture of changelessness and change, Baldovinetti is singularly representative of the Florentine Quattrocento, in which elements of the past and the future were so inextricably interwoven. It was inevitable that the borrowed rhythms of Byzantium, so perfect an expression of the religious sentiment and the sense of beauty of the East, should have been inadequate in an age when men's minds had turned again to those mental pursuits which had been abandoned for so long; that the spirit of investigation, already strong in other fields, should finally touch the graphic arts. . . . He was always searching for new ways of interpreting nature, new ways of setting down the painter's ideas, and yet he instinctively shrank from sacrificing to them that more decorative approach to painting which had characterized the art of his predecessors. In still another way, he is the most typical of the artists of his time. . . . The sculptors and painters of that time were still artisans, carefully distinguished as masters and journeymen to be sure, but men who rarely looked on painting frescoes and altarpieces as a nobler calling than painting furniture and shields and banners, and who made no such distinctions between painting, engraving and tarsia as would be made today. At least half of Baldovinetti's life was spent on work in other media than painting: on drawings for tarsias, on painted windows and on mosaics. His familiarity with these arts strongly affected his style in painting. . . .

He was a craftsman first and last, absorbed in the business of painting, but a craftsman with a genuine gift of pictorial imagination. By intuition he understood the importance of harmony and contrast, and by approaching the problem in a new way, he contrived new methods of achieving them. He also felt the need for simplification of structure and of background. Had he lived two hundred years earlier, he might have painted some such scenes as those which surround the beautiful and nameless painted cross in the Florentine Academy. Without any theory of uprights and horizontals, of parallels and correspondences of angles, he intuitively used these devices because he sensed their pictorial value. His desire for simplicity extended even to the modelling of hands and faces where all changes of plane are given the slightest possible indication. The preference for light rather than shadow, the delight in lines for their own sake, the predilection for surface pattern, not the gorgeous pattern of damask or brocade, but the simple forms of plane geometry, the search for the effective silhouette, all these things mark the taste which was the very marrow of his artistic endowment and which his education had never obliterated.

RUTH WEDGWOOD KENNEDY
Alesso Baldovinetti (1938)

Wood. Height 14⅞ in.; width 12½ in. (0.38 x 0.32). This Annunciation, probably painted between 1449 and 1454, may have formed part of the lost Saint Ansano altarpiece of 1450. It is close in style to the panels of the Silver Cupboard of Santissima Annunziata, executed by Baldovinetti c. 1449. Only twelve paintings on panel by this rare and important Florentine master are now known. Published by R. W. Kennedy (*Art in America*, 1940). Collections: Hartmann, Budapest; Mihalyffy, Budapest. *Kress Collection*, 1939.

SASSETTA · SIENESE 1392-1450

The Meeting of Saint Anthony and Saint Paul

Saint Paul fled into the desert. And when Saint Anthony in his turn repaired to the wilderness, thinking that he was the first hermit, he learned in a dream that another anchorite, better than himself, had a claim to his homage. Therefore Saint Anthony bent every effort to discover the whereabouts of this other hermit. And searching through the forests, he came first upon a hippocentaurus (centaur), half man and half horse, who told him to go to the right. Next he met an animal who was carrying some dates; the upper part of his body was that of a man, but he had the belly and the feet of a goat. Anthony asked him what he was; and he answered that he was a satyr, that is, one of those creatures which the pagans mistook for wood-gods. Finally Saint Anthony came face to face with a wolf, who led him to the cell where Saint Paul dwelt. But he, being aware of the approach of a man, had closed his door. Anthony besought him to open to him, declaring that he would die on the spot rather than go away. And Paul, yielding to his prayers, opened the door, and at once the two hermits embraced each other with great affection.

When the noon-hour drew near, a crow flew down, bearing a loaf formed of two halves. Anthony wondered at this, but Paul told him that God provided him daily with food in this manner: this day the quantity was doubled, on account of Anthony's visit. Thereupon they disputed piously over which of them was more worthy to divide the loaf. Paul wished that Anthony should do it, since he was the guest. Anthony insisted that it be Paul, who was the older. In the end both took hold of the loaf, and broke it in two.

As Anthony was on his way back to his cell, he saw two angels passing overhead, bearing the soul of Saint Paul. He hastened to retrace his steps, and found Paul's body kneeling in the attitude of prayer, so that Anthony thought he was still alive. But the saint was dead. And Anthony cried out: 'O blessed spirit, even in death thou showest still that which thou didst throughout thy life!' And while he was pondering over means of giving burial to Paul, thither came two lions, who dug a grave, helped to lay the body therein, and then returned to their forest. And Anthony took Paul's mantle, which was fashioned of palm-leaves; and thereafter he wore it on high feast days.

Jacobus de Voragine
Legenda aurea (c. 1255-66)

Wood. Height 18 in.; width 13⅝ in. (0.46 x 0.35). Painted c. 1432-1436. This panel formed part of a large altarpiece representing Saint Anthony Abbot and scenes from his life. Six other scenes have been identified as belonging probably to the same polyptych: Saint Anthony at Mass, in the Kaiser Friedrich Museum, Berlin; Saint Anthony Distributing his Money to the Poor, and the Departure of Saint Anthony from a Monastery, both in the Kress Collection, National Gallery of Art; the Temptation of Saint Anthony, and Saint Anthony and the Devils, both in the Jarves Collection, Yale University; and finally, Saint Anthony and the Porringer, in the Lehman Collection, New York. Collections: Viscount Allendale, London. *Kress Collection*, 1939.

ANDREA DEL CASTAGNO · FLORENTINE 1423-1457

The Youthful David

Curiosity about natural forms in all their variety and complexity — *naturalism* in the modern sense — first manifested itself in European art in Flanders, France, and North Italy about the second decade of the fifteenth century. It appears that Italy actually led the way in this movement, and that Lombardy was the point of origin. . . .

In Florence, too, this impulse was undoubtedly felt, but it is the great distinction of the Florentine artists that, however much their curiosity about particular forms may have been excited, their high intellectual passion for abstract ideas impelled them more to the study of some general principles underlying all appearance. They refused to admit the given facts of nature except in so far as they could become amenable to the generalising power of their art. Facts had to be digested into form before they were allowed into the system.

We can get an idea of what Florence of the fifteenth century meant for the subsequent tradition of European art if we consider that if it had not been for Florence the art of Italy might have been not altogether unlike the art of Flanders and the Rhine — a little more rhythmical, a little more gracious, perhaps, but fundamentally hardly more significant. . . .

Masaccio . . . . was helped perhaps by the fact that the new naturalism was as yet only a general perception of new aspects of natural form. It was left for his younger contemporaries to map out the new country methodically — to the group of adventurous spirits — Brunelleschi, Donatello, Castagno, and Uccello — who founded modern science, and gave to the understanding of classic art a methodical basis. It is in this group that the fierce intellectual passion of the Florentine genius manifests itself most clearly. Perspective and anatomy were the two studies which promised to reveal to them the secrets of natural form. The study of anatomy exemplifies mainly the aspect of curiosity, though even in this the desire to find the underlying principles of appearance is evident — on the other hand perspective, to its first discoverers, appeared to promise far more than an aid to verisimilitude, it may have seemed a visual revelation of the structure of space and through that a key to the construction of pictorial space. . . .

Neither perspective nor anatomy has any very immediate bearing upon art — both of them are means of ascertaining facts, and the question of art begins where the question of fact ends. But artists have always had to excite themselves with some kind of subsidiary intoxicant, and perspective and anatomy, while they were still in their infancy, acted admirably as stimulants. That they have by now become, for most artists, the dreariest of sedatives may make it difficult to conceive this. But at all events in that first generation they excited their devotees to an ardent search for abstract unity of design.

ROGER FRY
Vision and Design (1920)

Painted on a leather parade shield. Height 45 in.; width 32 in. above, 17 in. below (1.14 x 0.81 above, 0.43 below). Probably painted after 1450. Such shields were made to be carried in parades, at jousts or tournaments, but this is the only example painted by a great master which has come down to us. Not only is it unique but also Castagno's paintings are extremely rare. Apart from his frescoes in Florence and Venice, only four or five paintings by him have survived. Collections: Drury-Lowe, Locko Park, England. *Widener Collection*, 1942.

ANTONIO POLLAIUOLO · Florentine c. 1432-1498

Portrait of a Man

If nature had only one fixed standard for the proportions of the various parts, then the faces of all men would resemble each other to such a degree that it would be impossible to distinguish one from another; but she has varied the five parts of the face in such a way that although she has made an almost universal standard as to their size, she has not observed it in the various conditions to such a degree as to prevent one from being clearly distinguished from another. . . .

A picture or any representation of figures ought to be done in such a way that those who see them may be able with ease to recognise from their attitudes what is passing through their minds. So if you have to represent a man of good repute in the act of speaking, make his gestures accord with the probity of his speech; and similarly if you have to represent a brutal man, make him with fierce movements flinging out his arms towards his hearer, and the head and chest protruding forward beyond the feet should seem to accompany the hands of the speaker.

Just so a deaf mute who sees two people talking, although being himself deprived of the power of hearing, is none the less able to divine from the movements and gestures of the speakers the subject of their discussion.

· ·   ·   ·   ·

If you have a courtyard which, when you so please, you can cover over with a linen awning, the light will then be excellent. Or when you wish to paint a portrait, paint it in bad weather, at the fall of the evening, placing the sitter with his back to one of the walls of the courtyard. Notice in the streets at the fall of the evening when it is bad weather the faces of the men and women — what grace and softness they display! Therefore, O painter, you should have a courtyard fitted up with the walls tinted in black and with the roof projecting forward a little beyond the wall; and the width of it should be ten braccia, and the length twenty braccia, and the height ten braccia; and you should cover it over with the awning when the sun is on it, or else you should make your portrait at the hour of the fall of the evening when it is cloudy or misty, for the light then is perfect.

Leonardo da Vinci
Notebooks (c. 1483-1518)

Wood. Height 20½ in.; width 15¼ in. (0.52 x 0.39). This powerful example of Florentine portraiture traditionally was ascribed to Antonio Pollaiuolo, but most modern critics, with the exception of Berenson (*Italian Pictures of the Renaissance*), now give it to Castagno. Evidences for the correctness of the Pollaiuolo attribution, however, are to be found in the portrait's resemblance in draftsmanship to the embroideries in the Opera del Duomo, Florence, to the generally accepted Pollaiuolo drawing in the Albertina, Vienna, of Two Men Conversing, and to several of the archers in the Martyrdom of Saint Sebastian in the National Gallery, London. A generation separates this painting from the date of Leonardo's notebooks. Though Leonardo's remarks summarize the general principles of Renaissance portraiture, there is one important difference in style between the methods he advocates and those followed by Pollaiuolo and earlier artists. Leonardo recommends "grace" and "softness," an illumination "cloudy" and "misty," the type of lighting which encourages the indistinct, almost imperceptible gradations of modeling we find in the Mona Lisa. Pollaiuolo instead paints by a hard, clear light, models the separate planes of the figure with the sharp clarity of a relief in bronze. The difference between the sculptural approach of the Early Renaissance, as we find it in Pollaiuolo, and the pictorial methods of the High Renaissance, as described by Leonardo, is one of the most significant stylistic changes in the history of painting. Collections: Barone Cerbone del Nero, Florence; Marchese Torrigiani, Florence; Rodolphe Kann, Paris; J. Pierpont Morgan, New York. *Mellon Collection*, 1937.

PIERO DELLA FRANCESCA · UMBRIAN c. 1416-1492

Saint Apollonia

A natural, spontaneous, and unpretentious grandeur — this is the leading quality of all Piero's work. He is majestic without being at all strained, theatrical or hysterical — as Handel is majestic, not as Wagner. He achieves grandeur naturally with every gesture he makes, never consciously strains after it. Like Alberti, with whose architecture, as I hope to show, his painting has certain affinities, Piero seems to have been inspired by what I may call the religion of Plutarch's *Lives* — which is not Christianity, but a worship of what is admirable in man. Even his technically religious pictures are paeans in praise of human dignity. And he is everywhere intellectual. . . .

Aesthetically, Piero's work has this resemblance to Alberti's: that it too is essentially an affair of masses. What Alberti is to Brunelleschi, Piero della Francesca is to his contemporary, Botticelli. Botticelli was fundamentally a draughtsman, a maker of supple and resilient lines, thinking in terms of arabesques inscribed on the flat. Piero, on the contrary, has a passion for solidity as such. There is something in all his works that reminds one constantly of Egyptian sculpture. Piero has that Egyptian love of the smooth rounded surface that is the external symbol and expression of a mass. The faces of his personages look as though they were carved out of some very hard rock into which it had been impossible to engrave the details of a human physiognomy — the hollows, the lines and wrinkles of real life. They are ideal, like the faces of Egyptian gods and princes, surface meeting and marrying with curved unbroken surface in an almost geometrical fashion. Look, for example, at the faces of the women in Piero's fresco at Arezzo: 'The Queen of Sheba recognizing the Holy Tree.' They are all of one peculiar cast: the foreheads are high, rounded and smooth; the necks are like cylinders of polished ivory; from the midst of the concave sockets the eyelids swell out in one uninterrupted curve into convexity; the cheeks are unbrokenly smooth and the subtle curvature of their surfaces is indicated by a very delicate chiaroscuro which suggests more powerfully the solidity and mass of the flesh than the most spectacular Caravaggioesque light and shade could do.

Piero's passion for solidity betrays itself no less strikingly in his handling of the dresses and drapery of his figures. . . . Though transparent and of lawn, they hang round the heads of his women in stiff folds, as though they were made of steel. Among clothes he has a special fondness for pleated bodices and tunics. The bulge and recession of the pleated stuff fascinates him and he likes to trace the way in which the fluted folds follow the curve of the body beneath. . . .

I am attracted to his character by his intellectual power; by his capacity for unaffectedly making the grand and noble gesture; by his pride in whatever is splendid in humanity. And in the artist I find peculiarly sympathetic the lover of solidity, the painter of smooth curving surfaces, the composer who builds with masses. For myself I prefer him to Botticelli, so much so indeed, that if it were necessary to sacrifice all Botticelli's works in order to save the Resurrection, the Nativity, the Madonna della Misericordia and the Arezzo frescoes, I should unhesitatingly commit the Primavera and all the rest of them to the flames. It is unfortunate for Piero's reputation that his works should be comparatively few and in most cases rather difficult of access.

ALDOUS HUXLEY
Along the Road (1925)

Wood. Height 16¼ in.; width 11 in. (0.41 x 0.28). This panel apparently formed part of a polyptych, other parts of which were the Saint Clare and Saint Anthony in the Liechtenstein Gallery, Vienna. Possibly the polyptych was that of the Misericordia, Borgo San Sepolcro, now in the museum of that town and usually dated 1462. Collections: Santa Chiara, Borgo San Sepolcro; Casa Marini-Franceschi, Borgo San Sepolcro; Philip Lehman, New York. *Kress Collection*, 1939.

BOTTICELLI · FLORENTINE 1444-1510

The Adoration of the Magi

Botticelli lived in a generation of naturalists, and he might have been a mere naturalist among them. There are traces enough in his work of that alert sense of outward things, which, in the pictures of that period, fills the lawns with delicate living creatures, and the hillsides with pools of water, and the pools of water with flowering reeds. But this was not enough for him; he is a visionary painter, and in his visionariness he resembles Dante. Giotto, the tried companion of Dante, Masaccio, Ghirlandajo even, do but transcribe, with more or less refining, the outward image; they are dramatic, not visionary painters; they are almost impassive spectators of the action before them. But the genius of which Botticelli is the type usurps the data before it as the exponent of ideas, moods, visions of its own; in this interest it plays fast and loose with those data, rejecting some and isolating others, and always combining them anew. To him, as to Dante, the scene, the colour, the outward image or gesture, comes with all its incisive and importunate reality; but awakes in him, moreover, by some subtle law of his own structure, a mood which it awakes in no one else, of which it is the double or repetition, and which it clothes, that all may share it, with sensuous circumstance. . . .

He thus sets for himself the limits within which art, undisturbed by any moral ambition, does its most sincere and surest work. His interest is neither in the untempered goodness of Angelico's saints, nor the untempered evil of Orcagna's *Inferno;* but with men and women, in their mixed and uncertain condition, always attractive, clothed sometimes by passion with a character of loveliness and energy, but saddened perpetually by the shadow upon them of the great things from which they shrink. His morality is all sympathy; and it is this sympathy, conveying into his work somewhat more than is usual of the true complexion of humanity, which makes him, visionary as he is, so forcible a realist.

It is this which gives to his Madonnas their unique expression and charm. He has worked out in them a distinct and peculiar type, definite enough in his own mind, for he has painted it over and over again, sometimes one might think almost mechanically, as a pastime during that dark period when his thoughts were so heavy upon him.

WALTER PATER
The Renaissance (1888)

Wood. Height 27¾ in.; width 40⅝ in. (0.70 x 1.03). Horne (*Sandro Botticelli*) has suggested that this picture, which he considered the latest of all the extant Adorations by Botticelli, may be identified with a painting mentioned in the *Codice Magliabechiano* as having been executed in Rome. On stylistic grounds it is accepted by most critics as of Botticelli's Roman period, 1481-1482. Collections: Purchased in Rome by the engraver, Peralli, it was acquired in 1808 for the Hermitage Gallery, Leningrad, by Czar Alexander I. *Mellon Collection, 1937.*

PIERO DI COSIMO · FLORENTINE 1462 - c. 1521

The Visitation with Two Saints

And in truth, in all that there is to be seen by his hand, one recognizes a spirit very different and far distant from that of other painters, and a certain subtlety in the investigation of some of the deepest and most subtle secrets of Nature, without grudging time or labour, but only for his own delight and for his pleasure in the art. And it could not well be otherwise; since, having grown enamoured of her, he cared nothing for his own comfort, and reduced himself to eating nothing but boiled eggs, which, in order to save firing, he cooked when he was boiling his glue, and not six or eight at a time, but in fifties; and, keeping them in a basket, he would eat them one by one. In this life he found such peculiar pleasure that any other, in comparison with his own, seemed to him slavery. He could not bear the crying of children, the coughing of men, the sound of bells, and the chanting of friars; and when the rain was pouring in torrents from the sky, it pleased him to see it streaming straight down from the roofs and splashing on the ground. He had the greatest terror of lightning; and, when he heard very loud thunder, he wrapped himself in his mantle, and, having closed the windows and the door of the room, he crouched in a corner until the storm should pass. He was very varied and original in his discourse, and sometimes said such beautiful things, that he made his hearers burst with laughter. But when he was old, and near the age of eighty, he had become so strange and eccentric that nothing could be done with him. He would not have assistants standing round him, so that his misanthropy had robbed him of all possible aid. He was sometimes seized by a desire to work, but was not able, by reason of the palsy, and fell into such a rage that he tried to force his hands to labour; but, as he muttered to himself, the mahl-stick fell from his grasp, and even his brushes, so that it was pitiable to behold. Flies enraged him, and even shadows annoyed him.

In Florence, he painted many pictures for a number of citizens, which are dispersed among their various houses, and of such I have seen some that are very good; and so, also, various things for many other persons. . . . For the Chapel of Gino Capponi, in the Church of S. Spirito at Florence, he painted a panel wherein is the Visitation of Our Lady, with S. Nicholas, and a S. Anthony who is reading with a pair of spectacles on his nose, a very spirited figure. Here he counterfeited a book bound in parchment, somewhat old, which seems to be real, and also some balls that he gave to the S. Nicholas, shining and casting gleams of light and reflections from one to another; from which even by that time men could perceive the strangeness of his brain, and his constant seeking after difficulties.

GIORGIO VASARI
Le Vite de' piv eccellenti pittori, scvltori, e architettori (1568)

Wood. Height 72½ in.; width 74¼ in. (1.84 x 1.89). Painted for the chapel of Gino Capponi in Santo Spirito, Florence. Vasari refers to the picture on the right, which has been preserved exactly as he describes it. Drawings for the Visitation group and for several heads are in the Uffizi, Florence. The biblical text on the book in the hands of Saint Nicholas is taken from the Wisdom of Solomon (I, 1-5) "Love righteousness, ye that be judges of the earth. . . . For the holy spirit of discipline will flee deceit . . . . and will not abide when unrighteousness cometh in." Collections: Marchese Gaetano Capponi, Florence; Colonel W. Cornwallis-West, Newlands Manor, England. *Kress Collection*, 1939.

RAPHAEL · UMBRIAN 1483-1520

The Small Cowper Madonna

Raphael was aiming at beauty as much as were Alberti and Politian, and he tried as far as he could to keep his faces serene and quiet and free from the agitations of active feeling, so that his figures are epic rather than dramatic. That indefinable sense of quietude, of being deeply and truly satisfied, which we feel in the *Stanze* of Politian, which brings us nearer to the repose of Nature than the agitations of the human face, the "tranquil peace, without anything to trouble it," is what distinguished this ideal of lovely form — except that this peace of Raphael's is not "like unto that which is absorbed in God"; it is not a musical ideal, like Beatrice and Laura, but comes from the closest study of the real in its smallest details. We feel that the painter had a model before him, a model that sank into his imagination and fulfilled itself there, and acquired that purity and repose of form which he called "a certain idea." It is true that in this "certain idea" there is something of the classical, of the conventional, of the schools, but it is barely noticeable in these works of genius, sprung from a true inspiration, in which the feeling for beauty and the study of the real predominate. So the Madonnas of this century were born, Madonnas in whose faces there is nothing of the tremor, the abstraction, the ecstasy, of the saint, but only the simple and idyllic quietude of virginity and innocence. This type of face became more and more realistic, until in the Venetian imagination of Titian it took a form that is almost voluptuous.

The positive side of this movement is the ideal of form: form loved and studied as form, apart from content; and its negative side is precisely this indifference to content. With some of the men of the day it was a sort of eclecticism, as with Raphael, Leonardo da Vinci, Michelangelo, Ficino, Pico, who embraced all the contents, on the principle that all are a part of culture, of art, of thought — an eclecticism that in others was mixed with a gay satirizing, without acrimony, of the principles and forms and customs of the past that were still in good repute among the lower classes. The divine in this movement is the ideal of form, or, to put it differently, is culture taken by itself and deified. And even its comic and negative side is nothing more than a revelation of culture.

FRANCESCO DE SANCTIS
Storia della letteratura italiana (1870)

Wood. Height 23 in.; width 17 in. (0.59 x 0.44). Painted c. 1505 and probably just later than the Granduca Madonna in the Pitti, Florence. The present panel was considered by Morelli (*Italian Masters in German Galleries*), as "perhaps the most lovely of all Raphael's Madonnas." A drawing showing the whole composition in reverse is in the Uffizi, Florence; but whether this is a preliminary sketch or a contemporary copy after the painting remains in doubt. The building in the background is probably San Bernardino, a small church on the outskirts of Urbino, from which town this Madonna is said to have come. Collections: Purchased in Florence by Lord Cowper about 1780, the present painting remained in the possession of his family at Panshanger, Hertfordshire, until 1913. *Widener Collection*, 1942.

RAPHAEL · UMBRIAN 1483-1520

Saint George and the Dragon

This wonderful art can take us away from ourselves and give us, while we are under its spell, the feeling of being identified with the universe, perhaps even of being the soul of the universe. The feeling may be so conscious that it remains an artistic sensation — the most artistic of all; or it may transport one into the raptures of mysticism; but for those of us who are neither idolaters nor suppliants, this sense of identification with the universe is of the very essence of the religious emotion.

BERNHARD BERENSON
The Italian Painters of the Renaissance (1930)

Men's curiosity searches past and future
And clings to that dimension. But to apprehend
The point of intersection of the timeless
With time, is an occupation for the saint —
No occupation either, but something given
And taken, in a lifetime's death in love,
Ardour and selflessness and self-surrender.
For most of us, there is only the unattended
Moment, the moment in and out of time,
The distraction fit, lost in a shaft of sunlight,
The wild thyme unseen, or the winter lightning
Or the waterfall, or music heard so deeply
That it is not heard at all, but you are the music
While the music lasts. These are only hints and guesses,
Hints followed by guesses; and the rest
Is prayer, observance, discipline, thought and action.
The hint half guessed, the gift half understood, is
  Incarnation.

Here the impossible union
Of spheres of existence is actual,
Here the past and future
Are conquered, and reconciled,
Where action were otherwise movement
Of that which is only moved
And has in it no source of movement —
Driven by daemonic, chthonic
Powers. And right action is freedom
From past and future also.
For most of us, this is the aim
Never here to be realised;
Who are only undefeated
Because we have gone on trying;
We, content at the last
If our temporal reversion nourish
(Not too far from the yew-tree)
The life of significant soil.

T. S. ELIOT
Four Quartets (1943)

Wood. Height 11¼ in.; width 8⅜ in. (0.29 x 0.21). Painted 1504-1505. This is one of the most beautifully preserved of all Raphael's paintings on panel. It was commissioned by Duke Guidobaldo da Montefeltro, the ruler of Urbino, and taken as a gift to Henry VII of England by Count Baldassare Castiglione, author of *The Courtier*. (See quotation, page 54.) Raphael has depicted St. George wearing the insignia of the Order of the Garter to commemorate the bestowal of this honor on Duke Guidobaldo. On the horse's harness can be seen the signature of the artist, Raphello V, — the V standing for the first letter of the name of Raphael's birthplace, Urbino. The pen-and-ink drawing used originally as a tracing for the painting is in the Uffizi, Florence. Collections: From the English Royal Collection the panel passed into the possession of the Earl of Pembroke, and was engraved by L. Vosterman. Later it formed part of the Collection of Charles I, and was reproduced in tapestry at the royal factory at Mortlake. After the execution of Charles I the panel was taken to France, and was acquired from the Crozat Collection by Catherine the Great for the Hermitage Gallery, Leningrad. *Mellon Collection, 1937.*

RAPHAEL · UMBRIAN 1483-1520

The Alba Madonna

As in ancient Greece, so also in Renaissance Italy, the fine arts assumed the first place in the intellectual culture of the nation. But the thought and feeling of the modern world required an æsthetic medium more capable of expressing emotion in its intensity, variety, and subtlety than sculpture. Therefore painting was the art of arts for Italy. Yet even painting, notwithstanding the range and wealth of its resources, could not deal with the motives of Christianity so successfully as sculpture with the myths of Paganism. The religion it interpreted transcended the actual conditions of humanity, while art is bound down by its nature to the limitations of the world we live in. The Church imagined art would help her; and within a certain sphere of subjects, by vividly depicting Scripture histories and the lives of saints, by creating new types of serene beauty and pure joy, by giving form to angelic beings, by interpreting Mariolatry in all its charm and pathos, and by rousing deep sympathy with our Lord in His Passion, painting lent efficient aid to piety. Yet painting had to omit the very pith and kernel of Christianity as conceived by devout, uncompromising purists. Nor did it do what the Church would have desired. Instead of riveting the fetters of ecclesiastical authority, instead of enforcing mysticism and asceticism, it really restored to humanity the sense of its own dignity and beauty, and helped to prove the untenability of the mediæval standpoint; for art is essentially and uncontrollably free, and, what is more, is free precisely in that realm of sensuous delightfulness from which cloistral religion turns aside to seek her own ecstatic liberty of contemplation.

The first step in the emancipation of the modern mind was taken thus by art, proclaiming to men the glad tidings of their goodliness and greatness in a world of manifold enjoyment created for their use. Whatever painting touched, became by that touch human; piety, at the lure of art, folded her soaring wings and rested on the genial earth. This the Church had not foreseen. Because the freedom of the human spirit expressed itself in painting only under visible images, and not, like heresy, in abstract sentences; because this art sufficed for Mariolatry and confirmed the cult of local saints; because its sensuousness was not at variance with a creed that had been deeply sensualised —the painters were allowed to run their course unchecked.

JOHN ADDINGTON SYMONDS
Renaissance in Italy (1897)

Transferred from wood to canvas. Diameter 37¾ in. (0.96). Painted c. 1509 when Raphael, having just come to Rome, was beginning to show the influence of Michelangelo. Preliminary drawings for the tondo are in the Lille Museum. The painting was given, probably in 1528, to the Church of Monte Oliveto at Nocera de' Pagani. Taken to Spain at the end of the seventeenth century, it remained in the possession of the Dukes of Alba for more than a hundred years. Collections: Church of Monte Oliveto, Nocera de' Pagani near Naples; Don Gasparo de Haro y Guzman, Naples; the Duke of Alba, Madrid; Count Edmond Bourke, W. G. Coesvelt, London; The Hermitage Gallery, Leningrad. *Mellon Collection,* 1937.

RAPHAEL · UMBRIAN 1483-1520

Bindo Altoviti

The ancients excelled in beauty of form; Michael Angelo in grandeur of conception; Raphael in expression. In Raphael's faces, particularly his women, the expression is very superior to the form; in the ancient statues, the form is the principal thing. The interest which the latter excite, is in a manner external; it depends on a certain grace and lightness of appearance, joined with exquisite symmetry and refined susceptibility to voluptuous emotions; but there is in general a want of pathos. In their looks, we do not read the workings of the heart; by their beauty they seem raised above the sufferings of humanity, by their beauty they are deified. The pathos which they exhibit is rather that of present and physical distress, than of deep internal sentiment. What has been remarked of Leonardo da Vinci, is also true of Raphael, that there is an angelic sweetness and tenderness in his faces, in which human frailty and passion are purified by the sanctity of religion. The ancient statues are finer objects for the eye to contemplate; they represent a more perfect race of physical beings, but we have little sympathy with them. In Raphael, all our natural sensibilities are heightened and refined by the sentiments of faith and hope, pointing mysteriously to the interests of another world. The same intensity of passion appears also to distinguish Raphael from Michael Angelo. Michael Angelo's forms are grander, but they are not so informed with expression. Raphael's, however ordinary in themselves, are full of expression, "even to o'erflowing;" every nerve and muscle is impregnated with feeling, — bursting with meaning. In Michael Angelo, on the contrary, the powers of body and mind appear superior to any events that can happen to them; the capacity of thought and feeling is never full, never strained or tasked to the extremity of what it will bear. All is in a lofty repose and solitary grandeur, which no human interest can shake or disturb. It has been said, that Michael Angelo painted *man,* and Raphael *men;* that the one was an epic, the other a dramatic painter. But the distinction we have stated is, perhaps, truer and more intelligible, *viz.* that the one gave greater dignity of form, and the other greater force and refinement of expression.

WILLIAM HAZLITT
Fine Arts (1817)

Wood. Height 25⅞ in.; width 19¾ in. (0.66 x 0.50). Painted c. 1513. Bindo Altoviti was a Florentine banker, born in 1490, who lived for some time in Rome. He commissioned Raphael, according to Vasari, to paint two works, a religious picture, the Madonna dell' Impannata, now in the Pitti, Florence, and the present portrait. A bust of Bindo Altoviti as an older man, by Benvenuto Cellini, is in the Isabella Stewart Gardner Museum, Boston. Collections: The portrait remained in the Altoviti Palace, Florence, until 1808, when it was bought by Ludwig of Bavaria, later King Ludwig I, who presented it to the Alte Pinakothek in Munich. *Kress Collection,* 1939.

BERNARDINO LUINI · Milanese c. 1480-1532

The Illusion of Cephalus

Because Leonardo made models of machines, dug canals, built fortifications, and dissipated half his art-power in capricious ingenuities, we have many anecdotes of him; — but no picture of importance on canvas, and only a few withered stains of one upon a wall. But because his pupil, or reputed pupil, Luini, laboured in constant and successful simplicity, we have no anecdotes of him; — only hundreds of noble works. Luini is, perhaps, the best central type of the highly-trained Italian painter. He is the only man who entirely united the religious temper which was the spirit-life of art, with the physical power which was its bodily life. He joins the purity and passion of Angelico to the strength of Veronese: the two elements, poised in perfect balance, are so calmed and restrained, each by the other, that most of us lose the sense of both. The artist does not see the strength, by reason of the chastened spirit in which it is used; and the religious visionary does not recognize the passion, by reason of the frank human truth with which it is rendered. He is a man ten times greater than Leonardo; — a mighty colourist, while Leonardo was only a fine draughtsman in black, staining the chiaroscuro drawing, like a coloured print: he perceived and rendered the delicatest types of human beauty that have been painted since the days of the Greeks, while Leonardo depraved his finer instincts by caricature, and remained to the end of his days the slave of an archaic smile: and he is a designer as frank, instinctive, and exhaustless as Tintoret, while Leonardo's design is only an agony of science, admired chiefly because it is painful, and capable of analysis in its best accomplishment. Luini has left nothing behind him that is not lovely; but of his life I believe hardly anything is known beyond remnants of tradition which murmur about Lugano and Saronno, and which remain ungleaned. This only is certain, that he was born in the loveliest district of North Italy, where hills, and streams, and air, meet in softest harmonies. Child of the Alps, and of their divinest lake, he is taught, without doubt or dismay, a lofty religious creed, and a sufficient law of life, and of its mechanical arts. Whether lessoned by Leonardo himself, or merely one of many, disciplined in the system of the Milanese school, he learns unerringly to draw, unerringly and enduringly to paint. His tasks are set him without question day by day, by men who are justly satisfied with his work, and who accept it without any harmful praise, or senseless blame. Place, scale, and subject are determined for him on the cloister wall or the church dome; as he is required, and for sufficient daily bread, and little more, he paints what he has been taught to design wisely, and has passion to realize gloriously: every touch he lays is eternal, every thought he conceives is beautiful and pure: his hand moves always in radiance of blessing; from day to day his life enlarges in power and peace; it passes away cloudlessly, the starry twilight remaining arched far against the night.

JOHN RUSKIN
The Queen of the Air (1869)

Fresco transferred to canvas. Height 89¾ in.; width 49 in. (2.28 x 1.25). This painting, in which Cephalus is described as haunted by apparitions of his murdered wife and her dog, Laelaps, is the sixth scene in a series of nine frescoes depicting the story of Cephalus and Procris, now in the National Gallery of Art, Kress Collection. They were painted about 1507, as part of the decorations of the Villa Pelucca at San Sepolcro, near Milan. Vasari, who saw the frescoes in 1560, states that Luini painted "the house of Signor Gian Francesco Rabbia — that is, the façade, loggie, halls and apartments — depicting there many of the Metamorphoses of Ovid and other fables, with good and beautiful figures, executed with much delicacy." The remains of these frescoes are now scattered among a number of other museums: the Brera, Milan; Palazzo Reale, Milan; Louvre, Paris; Kaiser Friedrich Museum, Berlin, and in several private collections. Collections: Villa Pelucca, San Sepolcro; Michele Cavalieri, Milan; Henri Cernuschi, Rodolphe Kann, Paris. *Kress Collection*, 1939.

ERCOLE ROBERTI · FERRARESE c. 1456-1496

Giovanni II Bentivoglio

I look upon the true and principal Profession of a Courtier to consist in the Skill of Arms, which I would have him exercise with much Life and Activity; and to be distinguish'd among others for his Bravery, and Courage, and Fidelity. . . .

Let him converse with all with Chearfulness and Familiarity, and not decline such Amusements as others engage in; provided he refuse not at any time a commendable Action, and govern himself with so much Judgment, as not to be guilty of what would make him ridiculous. Let him laugh, joke, and dance, but always in such a manner as shall discover both his Wit and his Discretion, and let his Conversation and Actions be attended with a certain Grace and Dignity. . . .

The Courtier ought to set off all his Actions, Gestures, and Habits, and every Motion with a Grace: And this you seem to apply as a Sawce for everything, without which all his other Virtues and Qualifications would be of small Account. And I am verily persuaded that every Man would soon be convinced thereof, for by Virtue of the Expression we may affirm, that whosoever hath Grace is gracious. . . .

What therefore is the principal and most necessary Ingredient for a Courtier, in Order to his writing and speaking well, in my Opinion, is Knowledge and Understanding: For unless he comprehend the Subject well, which he proposes to treat of, he can neither speak or write to any Purpose. Then must he range it in good Method and Order, and afterward endeavour to cloath it in beautiful Expressions. . . .

I return again to our Courtier: Whom in Letters I would have to be more than moderately instructed, especially in what they style Polite Literature, and to understand not only the Latin Tongue but the Greek, because of the Variety of Things which are written in it with great Accuracy and Beauty. . . .

I am not satisfied with our Courtier, unless he be a Master of Musick: And beside his Understanding to play by Book, have Skill likewise in Variety of Instruments. . . .

Our Courtier ought to have some Skill in Painting, since it is attended with such Credit and Advantage, and more valued in those Days, when Men were more eminent and remarkable for their Courage than they are at present. And though he never reap any other Profit or Pleasure from it, (besides the Help it gives him to judge of the Excellency of Statues, both Ancient and Modern, of Vessels, Buildings, Medals, Gravings, and such like,) it gives him a better Taste and Knowledge of living Beauty.

BALDASSARE CASTIGLIONE
Il Cortegiano (1528)

Wood. Height 21⅛ in.; width 15 in. (0.54 x 0.38). Painted c. 1480. The identity of the sitter and his wife (whose portrait is on page 57) is established by their portraits included in Lorenzo Costa's altarpiece, dated 1488, in San Giacomo Maggiore, Bologna. The present panels are probably the most distinguished examples of Ferrarese portraiture. Collections: Charles Timbal, Gustave Dreyfus, Paris. *Kress Collection,* 1939.

ERCOLE ROBERTI · Ferrarese c. 1456-1496

Ginevra Bentivoglio

Ginevra, distinguished wife of the famous Golden Knight, Giovanni Bentivoglio, Prince of Bologna, and daughter of Alessandro Sforza, Lord of Pesaro, shines by her many virtues and must be mentioned among the famous ladies of our time. Through the great light of the virtues which shine within her, she is an ornament to the City of Bologna, mother of students. In the first place she is famous for her very elegant appearance, gestures and carriage. She moves with a composure which is truly regal. Having lost her first husband and married again, she proved extremely fecund and has already borne sixteen handsome children, both boys and girls. She has a certain remarkable charm in her face and a certain gravity of expression equal to her charm. Her prudence and intelligence are even greater, and beauty of manners is her constant adornment. She speaks with exceeding probity and simple modesty. In all her actions, whether standing, walking, or sitting, she evinces the greatest grace and composure. She does not forget favors, is always grateful, generous and gentle in her speech. She is indeed most affable in entertaining her friends and kinsmen, and is extremely obliging and polite. In her you may see a certain domestic modesty and uncorrupted self-restraint. She loves and cultivates solitude rather than public gatherings, remaining secluded at home most of the time in the manner of pious people. There she occupies herself with religion, nor does she despise secular literature. She takes pleasure in frequently hearing about those women who have acquired fame because of their virtues. She hates and despises shameful words and ignoble talk. She worships God most devoutly, particularly in that she prefers to frequent holy places. She is most charitable towards the servants of Christ and the poor, nor is she any the less diligent in her prayers to God and frequent homage to the Saints. She most ardently listens to the word of God and holds it in her heart above all things, so that other women beholding her example are easily encouraged to imitate and to follow in her footsteps. She is moderate in eating and drinking and does not dress sumptuously. She takes delight in association with those persons who are distinguished for their modesty. In all her doings this great woman shows to a remarkable degree the qualities which all are wont to require of a ruler. . . . For this reason we have decided to write down this account of her outstanding virtues so that any woman desirous of moral comeliness and fame, and anxious to obtain the favor of God, may read of her virtues and may not refuse or be unwilling to imitate her example, through which life may be made more joyful and immortality assured.

Jacobus Philippus Bergomensis
De Claris Mulieribus (1497)

Wood. Height 21⅛ in.; width 15¼ in. (0.54 x 0.39). For date and provenance see note on page 54. Ginevra Bentivoglio was the sister of the Duchess of Urbino. The Duke of Urbino had commissioned Piero della Francesca to paint the double portrait of himself and his wife, now in the Uffizi, Florence, and it seems probable that Bentivoglio, the tyrant of Bologna, impressed with the fame of the Piero della Francesca double portrait, desired that he and his consort should be similarly commemorated. *Kress Collection*, 1939.

ANDREA MANTEGNA · PADUAN 1431-1506

Judith with the Head of Holofernes

All thoughts and emotions are inter-dependent. In the words of the dear old song,

> The roses round the door
> Make me love mother more.

One feeling is excited by another. Our faculties work best in a congenial emotional atmosphere. For example, Mantegna's faculty for making noble arrangements of forms was stimulated by his feelings about heroic and god-like humanity. Expressing those feelings, which he found exciting, he also expressed — and in the most perfect manner of which he was capable — his feelings about masses, surfaces, solids, and voids. "The roses round the door" — his hero worship — "made him love mother more" — made him, by stimulating his faculty for composition, paint better. If Isabella d'Este had made him paint apples, table napkins and bottles, he would have produced, being uninterested in these objects, a poor composition. And yet, from a purely formal point of view, apples, bottles and napkins are quite as interesting as human bodies and faces. But Mantegna — and with him the majority of painters — did not happen to be very passionately interested in these inanimate objects. When one is bored one becomes boring.

> The apples round the door
> Make me a frightful bore.

Inevitably; unless I happen to be so exclusively interested in form that I can paint anything that has a shape; or unless I happen to possess some measure of that queer pantheism, that animistic superstition which made Van Gogh regard the humblest of common objects as being divinely or devilishly alive. *"Crains dans le mur aveugle un regard qui t'épie."* If a painter can do that, he will be able, like Van Gogh, to make pictures of cabbage fields and the bedrooms of cheap hotels that shall be as wildly dramatic as a Rape of the Sabines.

ALDOUS HUXLEY
Along the Road (1925)

Wood. Height 12 in.; width 7⅛ in. (0.31 x 0.18). Painted probably after 1490. The theme of Judith and Holofernes was treated frequently by Mantegna and his school. Numerous drawings of this subject exist, among them one in the Uffizi, Florence, dated 1491, and another in the Kress Collection, National Gallery of Art. The painting reproduced on the right may have formed part of a series of Old Testament stories, the theme of which was probably The Triumph of Woman. A grisaille showing the same subject, with the composition in reverse, is in the National Gallery, Ireland. This grisaille formed part of a series, of which two other panels, representing Samson and Delilah and the Judgment of Solomon, have been preserved. Collections: Charles I gave the panel to Lord Pembroke, in exchange for paintings by Bellini and Parmigiano. It remained in the Pembroke Collection, Wilton House, until brought to America. *Widener Collection,* 1942.

GIOVANNI BELLINI · Venetian c. 1430-1516

Portrait of a Condottiere

War being an occupation by which a man cannot support himself with honour at all times, ought not to be followed as a business by any but princes or governors of commonwealths; and if they are wise men they will not suffer any of their subjects or citizens to make that their only profession. Indeed no good man ever did; for surely he cannot be called a good man, who exercises an employment that obliges him to be rapacious, fraudulent and cruel, at all times, in order to support himself; as all those must be of course, of what rank soever they are, who make a trade of war, because it will not maintain them in time of peace; upon which account, they are under a necessity either of endeavoring to prevent a peace, or of taking all means to make such provisions for themselves in time of war, that they may not want sustenance when it is over. But neither of these courses is consistent with common honesty; for whoever resolves to heap as much in time of war as will support him for ever after, must be guilty of robbery, murder, and many other acts of violence upon his friends as well as his enemies; and in endeavouring to prevent a peace, commanders must have recourse to many pitiful tricks and artifices to deceive those that employ them. But if they fail in their designs, and find they cannot prevent a peace, as soon as their pay is stopped, and they can live no longer in the licentious manner they used to do, they set up for soldiers of fortune, and having got a parcel of their disbanded men together, make no scruple of plundering a whole country without mercy or distinction. You must have heard that when the late wars were over in Italy, and the country full of disbanded soldiers, they formed themselves into several bands, and went about plundering some towns and laying others under contribution. You must likewise have read how the Carthaginian soldiers (after the first war was ended in which they had been engaged with the Romans) assembled together under the banners of Matho and Spendius (two officers whom they had chosen in a tumultuary manner to command them) and made a more dangerous war upon their own country, than that which had been just concluded. . . . Such evils, and others of the like nature, are owing to men who make war their only occupation; according to the proverb, *war makes thieves, and peace hangs them;* for those that know not how to get their bread any other way, when they are disbanded, finding nobody that has occasion for their service, and disdaining the thoughts of living in poverty and obscurity, are forced to have recourse to such ways of supporting themselves as generally bring them to the gallows.

NICCOLÒ MACHIAVELLI
Arte della guerra (1520)

Wood. Height 20 in.; width 14½ in. (0.51 x 0.37). Painted 1480-1490. The traditional identification of the sitter in this austere portrait is the Venetian condottiere, Colleoni, whose statue by Verrocchio is well known. Colleoni, however, died in 1475, and the present painting can scarcely be earlier than 1480, which is the approximate date given to it by Gronau (*Giovanni Bellini*). Von Hadeln (*Burlington Magazine*, 1927) believes it to be not earlier than 1500. The military air of the sitter is unmistakable, and it is entirely possible that another Venetian leader is here represented. Gronau tentatively suggests that the present picture may be identified with a small portrait by Giovanni Bellini of Jacomo Marcello, Captain-General of the Army, which Michiel (the Anonimo Morelliano) saw in the Marcello Palace, Venice, in the sixteenth century. Collections: The painting was bought in Venice in 1786 by Sir Abraham Hume and passed through his descendants to the Collection of Earl Brownlow, Ashridge Park, England. *Kress Collection*, 1939.

GIOVANNI BELLINI · VENETIAN C. 1430-1516

The Feast of the Gods

Turrigera frontem Cybele redimita corona
  convocat aeternos ad sua festa deos.
convocat et satyros et, rustica numina, nymphas;
  Silenus, quamvis nemo vocarat, adest.
nec licet et longum est epulas narrare deorum:
  in multo nox est pervigilata mero.
hi temere errabant in opacae vallibus Idae,
  pars iacet et molli gramine membra levat,
hi ludunt, hos somnus habet, pars brachia nectit
  et viridem celeri ter pede pulsat humum.
Vesta iacet placidamque capit secura quietem,
  sicut erat, positum caespite fulta caput.

Cybele, with her brow crowned with turrets, invites to her feast the eternal Gods. She invites, too, the Satyrs and the Nymphs, Deities of the country. Silenus comes, *too,* though no one had invited him. It is not lawful, 'twere tedious, too, to relate the banquet of the Gods; a sleepless night is spent over copious draughts of wine. Some are carelessly wandering in the vales of the shady Ida; some are lying down, and resting their limbs on the soft herbage. Some are disporting: upon some, Sleep lays her hand: some join hands, and then with active foot they beat the ground. Vesta is lying down, and, free from fear, she enjoys quiet repose, supporting her head, reclining just as it was, on a tuft of grass.

OVID
Fasti (c. 7 A.D.)

In the year 1514 Duke Alfonso of Ferrara had caused a little chamber to be decorated, and had commissioned Dosso . . . . and he desired that there should also be there pictures by the hand of Gian Bellini. Bellini painted on another wall a vat of red wine with some Bacchanals around it, and Satyrs, musicians, and other men and women, all drunk with wine, and near them a nude and very beautiful Silenus, riding on his ass, with figures about him that have the hands full of fruits and grapes; which work was in truth executed and coloured with great diligence, insomuch that it is one of the most beautiful pictures that Gian Bellini ever painted. . . . On that vat Gian Bellini wrote these words: JOANNES BELLINUS VENETUS, P. 1514. That work he was not able to finish completely, because he was old, and Tiziano, as the most excellent of all the others, was sent for to the end that he might finish it.

GIORGIO VASARI
*Le Vite de' piv eccellenti pittori,
scvltori, e architettori* (1568)

Canvas. Height 67 in.; width 74 in. (1.70 x 1.88). Signed, and dated. Vasari's statement that the picture was completed by Titian was apparently suggested by the fact that parts of the drapery and foliage seem to be reworked, and also that Titian painted for the same chamber in Alfonso's castle three other Bacchanals of almost identical size, now in the Prado, Madrid, and the National Gallery, London. The pictures in the Prado are based upon Philostratus, while it has been pointed out recently by Dr. Edgar Wind that the present picture and the Bacchanal in the National Gallery, London, are based upon passages from the *Fasti* of Ovid (I, 391 ff., VI, 319 ff. and III, 507 ff). In the following century, Nicolas Poussin was so impressed by Bellini's Feast of the Gods that he made the famous copy now in the National Gallery of Scotland. Collections: Duke Alfonso d'Este, Ferrara; Cardinal Pietro Aldobrandini, Vincenzo Camuccini, Rome; Duke of Northumberland, Alnwick Castle. *Widener Collection,* 1942.

GIORGIONE · VENETIAN c. 1478-1510

The Adoration of the Shepherds

The beginnings of Venetian painting link themselves to the last, stiff, half-barbaric splendours of Byzantine decoration, and are but the introduction into the crust of marble and gold on the walls of the *Duomo* of Murano, or of Saint Mark's, of a little more of human expression. And throughout the course of its later development, always subordinate to architectural effect, the work of the Venetian school never escaped from the influence of its beginnings. Unassisted, and therefore unperplexed, by naturalism, religious mysticism, philosophical theories, it had no Giotto, no Angelico, no Botticelli. Exempt from the stress of thought and sentiment, which taxed so severely the resources of the generations of Florentine artists, those earlier Venetian painters, down to Carpaccio and the Bellini, seem never for a moment to have been tempted even to lose sight of the scope of their art in its strictness, or to forget that painting must be before all things decorative, a thing for the eye, a space of colour on the wall, only more dexterously blent than the marking of its precious stone or the chance interchange of sun and shade upon it. . . . At last, with final mastery of all the technical secrets of his art, and with somewhat more than "a spark of the divine fire to his share," comes Giorgione. He is the inventor of *genre,* of those easily movable pictures which serve for uses, neither of devotion, nor of allegorical or historical teaching — little groups of real men and women, amid congruous furniture or landscape — morsels of actual life, conversation or music or play, refined upon or idealised, till they come to seem like glimpses of life from afar. Those spaces of more cunningly blent colour, obediently filling their places, hitherto, in a mere architectural scheme, Giorgione detaches from the wall; he frames them by the hands of some skilful carver, so that people may move them readily and take with them where they go, like a poem in manuscript, or a musical instrument, to be used, at will, as a means of self-education, stimulus or solace, coming like an animated presence, into one's cabinet, to enrich the air as with some choice aroma, and, like persons, live with us, for a day or a lifetime. Of all art like this, art which has played so large a part in men's culture since that time, Giorgione is the initiator. Yet in him too that old Venetian clearness or justice, in the apprehension of the essential limitations of the pictorial art, is still undisturbed; and, while he interfuses his painted work with a high-strung sort of poetry, caught directly from a singularly rich and high-strung sort of life, yet in his selection of subject, or phase of subject, in the subordination of mere subject to pictorial design, to the main purpose of a picture, he is typical of that aspiration of all the arts towards music, which I have endeavoured to explain, — towards the perfect identification of matter and form.

WALTER PATER
The Renaissance (1888)

Wood. Height 35¾ in.; width 43½ in. (0.91 x 1.11). Painted 1500-1505. In the correspondence between Isabella d'Este and Taddeo Albano in 1510, two paintings representing *"una Nocte"* (i. e. Nativities or Adorations) by Giorgione are mentioned in Venetian collections. It is possible that the present Adoration, one of the great achievements of Venetian painting, is referred to in these letters. It is also possible that this is the painting mentioned in Bordone's appraisal of the Grimani Collection in 1563 and in the catalogue of the English Royal Collections by Bathoe in 1758. However, the first certain mention of the picture is in 1841, as belonging to the Collection of Cardinal Fesch in Rome. A drawing in Windsor closely related to the painting is reproduced by Von Hadeln. Collections: After the sale of the Collection of Cardinal Fesch in Rome in 1841, the painting passed into the possession of Claudius Tarral. It was sold in 1847 to T. Wentworth Beaumont, and passed by inheritance to Lord Allendale, London. *Kress Collection*, 1939.

TITIAN · VENETIAN c. 1477-1576

Allegory (Alfonso d'Este and Laura Diante?)

Gusto in art is power or passion defining any object. — It is not so difficult to explain this term in what relates to expression (of which it may be said to be the highest degree) as in what relates to things without expression, to the natural appearances of objects, as mere colour or form. The truth is, that there is hardly any object entirely devoid of expression, without some character of power belonging to it, some precise association with pleasure or pain; and it is in giving this truth of character from the truth of feeling, whether in the highest or the lowest degree, but always in the highest degree of which the subject is capable, that gusto consists.

There is a gusto in the colouring of Titian. Not only do his heads seem to think — his bodies seem to feel. This is what the Italians mean by the *morbidezza* of his flesh-colour. It seems sensitive and alive all over; not merely to have the look and texture of flesh, but the feeling in itself. For example, the limbs of his female figures have a luxurious softness and delicacy, which appears conscious of the pleasure of the beholder. As the objects themselves in nature would produce an impression on the sense, distinct from every other object, and having something divine in it, which the heart owns and the imagination consecrates, the objects in the picture preserve the same impression, absolute, unimpaired, stamped with all the truth of passion, the pride of the eye, and the charms of beauty. Rubens makes his flesh-colour like flowers, Albano's is like ivory, Titian's is like flesh, and like nothing else. It is as different from that of other painters, as the skin is from a piece of white or red drapery thrown over it. The blood circulates here and there, the blue veins just appear, the rest is distinguished throughout only by that sort of tingling sensation to the eye, which the body feels within itself. This is gusto. — Vandyke's flesh-colour, though it has great truth and purity, wants gusto. It has not the internal character, the living principle in it. It is a smooth surface, not a warm, moving mass. It is painted without passion, with indifference. The hand only has been concerned. The impression slides off from the eye, and does not, like the tones of Titian's pencil, leave a sting behind it in the mind of the spectator. The eye does not acquire a taste or appetite for what it sees. In a word, gusto in painting is where the impression made on one sense excites by affinity those of another.

WILLIAM HAZLITT
The Examiner (May 26, 1816)

Canvas. Height 36 in.; width 32¼ in. (0.91 x 0.82). Painted 1515-1525. A composition found with variations in two other paintings, one in the Louvre, Paris, and the other in the Cambo Collection, Barcelona. The woman is portrayed nude only in this example. It has been suggested that she may represent Laura Diante, and the man Alfonso d'Este. Some critics, however, have recognized in the figure of the man a portrait of Federigo Gonzaga, and in the woman a generalized type of feminine beauty. If Federigo is represented, the painting belongs doubtless to the artist's Mantuan period (c. 1525); if Alfonso, to his Ferrarese period (1516-1523). The painting, according to tradition, remained in Ferrara from Renaissance times, and is recorded in 1800 as in the Collection of Conte Leopoldo Cicognara in Ferrara. Collections: Benacosi Collection, Ferrara; Conte Leopoldo Cicognara, Ferrara; Comte de Pourtalès-Gorgier, Paris; Baron Michel Lazzaroni, Paris; Henry Goldman Collection, New York. *Kress Collection*, 1939.

TITIAN · Venetian c. 1477-1576

Venus and Adonis

Those people are mistaken, in my judgment, who praise the admirable Titian by saying that he uses color well. If he merited no other praise but this, many a woman would surpass him. They certainly paint their faces so beautifully in white and vermilion that, as to the appearance of the colors, men are deceived by them. But if they have a long nose, a large mouth, or if their eyes, those seats of grace and beauty, are squinting or badly formed, the tints of those colors do not hide the ugliness or deformity. So the praiseworthiness in painting lies principally in the disposition of the forms so as to discover the beauty and the perfection of nature. In this, as in all other respects, the most excellent Titian is not merely divine after the manner of the world's opinion, but supremely divine and without equal as one who couples perfection of draftsmanship with liveliness of coloring to such an extent that his forms seem not painted, but real. The painter must have another quality not less necessary than all the rest: that is, the paintings he makes should so move the emotions and passions of the soul, that those who behold them are either delighted or perturbed, according to the subject, as with the works of good poets and orators. The statue of the Laocoön, which is in the Belvedere at Rome, may serve us as an example of this quality in the ancient artists. It is likewise fitting that the flesh tints be relatively delicate and soft, according to the character of the figure. For greater softness characterizes the flesh of a woman than of a man, of a youth than of an old man, of a gentleman than of a peasant, of a man accustomed to live in peace and delicately than of a soldier used to feats of arms, and so on. And the tints ought likewise to be varied as nature varies them. Just as an extreme white never pleases, so a certain tempering between white and brown contains every gradation of charm, as one sees in the Saint Catherine of our great Titian, which is in San Niccolò dei Frati Minori. Yet, on the contrary, that great diversity of colors affected by most painters today lacks verisimilitude, although it is recognized as valuable in giving relief to the figures, and delights the eyes of the ignorant. . . .

Yet, whoever establishes his art on such theories cannot go wrong; while on the contrary an infinity of painters err who do not realize these things. By rudely daubing a canvas or a panel with a portrait, or several figures done rather according to longstanding practice than to reason or art, they expect not only to be considered most excellent masters, but to surpass Raphael, Michelangelo, and Titian. And when they are not appreciated, they lament not their ignorance, but fortune, as happens also to many of us writers.

Lodovico Dolce
Letter to Gaspero Ballini (c. 1559)

Canvas. Height 42 in.; width 53 in. (1.07 x 1.35). Painted after 1560. Of the several versions of this theme by Titian, the present painting is considered the last executed by him, and in many ways his most successful treatment of the subject. Collections: Originally in the Barbarigo Palace, Venice, it was purchased in the seventeenth century by Lord Bristol. The diarist, Evelyn, records having seen it in 1679 in the home of the Countess of Bristol and again in 1685, when it had passed by inheritance to Lady Sunderland. Later it entered the collection of Earl Spencer and remained in the possession of his descendants until it was brought to America. *Widener Collection*, 1942.

LORENZO LOTTO · VENETIAN c. 1480-1556

Allegory

Michael Angelo here paused for breath, and Zapata began. . . .

Pray, Signor Michael . . . . explain a doubt of mine about the art of painting: why is it that artists sometimes, as we see in many parts of this city, paint a thousand monsters and animals, some of them with a woman's face and the lower parts and tail of a fish, others with the arms of tigers and with wings, or with a man's face; anything in fact that delights the painter's fancy and has never existed.

I shall be glad, said Michael, to tell you why it is the custom to paint things that have never existed and how reasonable is this licence and how it accords with the truth; for some critics, not understanding the matter, are wont to say that Horace, the lyric poet, wrote those lines in dispraise of painters:

> Pictoribus atque poetis
> Quidlibet audendi semper fuit aequa potestas:
> Scimus, et hanc veniam petimusque damusque vicissim.

And in this sentence he does in nowise blame painters but praises and favours them, since he says that poets and painters have licence to dare, that is to dare do what they choose. And this insight and power they have always had; for whenever (as very rarely happens) a great painter makes a work which seems to be artificial and false, this falseness is truth; and greater truth in that place would be a lie. For he will not paint anything that cannot exist according to its nature; he will not paint a man's hand with ten fingers, nor paint a horse with the ears of a bull or a camel's hump . . . . for all such things are most false. But if, in order to observe what is proper to a time and place, he exchange the parts or limbs (as in grotesque work which would otherwise be very false and insipid) and convert a griffin or a deer downwards into a dolphin or upwards into any shape he may choose, putting wings in place of arms, and cutting away the arms if wings are more suitable, this converted limb, of lion or horse or bird, will be most perfect according to its nature; and this may seem false but can really only be called ingenious or monstrous. And sometimes it is more in accordance with reason to paint a monstrosity (to vary and relax the senses and the object presented to men's eyes, since sometimes they desire to see what they have never seen and think cannot exist) rather than the ordinary figure, admirable though it be, of man or animals. And . . . . it may be really great work if it is made by a skilful artist.

FRANCISCO DE HOLLANDA
Quatro Dialogos sobre a pintura (1548)

Wood. Height 22¼ in.; width 17⅛ in. (0.57 x 0.44). Painted 1505. This panel is a cover for the portrait of Bernardo Rossi of Treviso, now in the Naples Museum. The content of the painting reflects an aspect of Renaissance Humanistic thought. The left half, where a cupid examines evidences of intellectual pursuits, possibly may be taken to represent the contemplative side of life, while the right half, where a satyr drinks from a silver ewer, may symbolize the sensual side. In the background, a winged figure climbs a steep path, perhaps denoting the spirit ascending to the light of reason. The lines quoted above from Horace may be translated: "Painters and poets always have enjoyed unlimited license; we know this and we claim for ourselves the same liberty, and grant it to others." Collections: Giacomo Gritti, Bergamo, Italy. *Kress Collection*, 1939.

DOSSO DOSSI · FERRARESE c. 1479-c. 1542

Circe and Her Lovers in a Landscape

"What is the true *content* of art, and with what aim is that content brought before us?" On this head we are confronted by the common opinion that it is the task and object of art to bring before our sense, feeling, and power of emulation *every thing* that the spirit of man can perceive or conceive. Art has in short to realize for us the well-known saying, *"Nihil humani a me alienum puto."* Its object is therefore declared to be that of arousing and giving life to slumbering emotions, inclinations, passions of *every* description, of filling the heart up to the brim; of compelling man-kind, whether cultured or the reverse, to pass through all that the human soul carries in its most intimate and mysterious chambers, all that it is able to experience and reproduce, all that the heart is able to stir and evoke in its depths and its countlessly manifold possibilities; and yet further to deliver to the domain of feeling and the delight of our vision all that the mind may possess of essen-tial and exalted being in its thought and the Idea — that majestic hierarchy of the noble, eternal, and true; and no less to interpret for us misfortune and misery, wickedness and crime; to make the hearts of men realize through and through all that is atrocious and dreadful, no less than every kind of pleasure and blessedness; and last of all to start the imagination like a rover among the day-dream playing-fields of the fancy, there to revel in the seductive mirage of visions and emotions which cap-tivate the senses. All this infinitely manifold content — so it is held — it is the function of art to explore, in order that by this means the experience of our external life may be repaired of its defi-ciencies, and yet from a further point of view that the passions we share with all men may be excited, not merely that the experiences of life may not have us unmoved, but that we ourselves may there-after long to make ourselves open channels of a universal experience. Such a stimulus is not pre-sented on the plane of actual experience itself, but can only come through the semblance of it, that is to say through the illusions which art, in its creations, substitutes for the actual world. And the possibility of such a deception, by means of the semblances of art, depends on the fact that all reality must for man pass through the medium of the vision and imaginative idea; and it is only after such a passage that it penetrates the emotional life and the will. In such a process it is of no consequence whether it is immediate external reality which claims his attention, or whether the result is effected by some other way, in other words by means of images, symbols, and ideas, which contain and dis-play the content of such actuality. Men are able to imagine things, which do not actually exist, as if they did exist. Consequently it is precisely the same thing for our emotional life, whether it is the objective world or merely the show of the same, in virtue of which a situation, a relation, or any con-tent of life, in short, is brought home to us. Either mode is equally able to stir in us an echo to the essential secret which it carries, whether it be in grief or joy, in agitation or convulsion, and can cause to flow through us the feelings and passions of anger, hate, pity, anxiety, fear, love, reverence and admiration, honour and fame.

G. W. F. HEGEL
Aesthetik (1835)

Canvas. Height 39½ in.; width 53⅜ in. (1.00 x 1.36). Painted about 1514 or 1516, in which year — according to Vasari — Duke Alfonso of Ferrara had caused a little chamber to be decorated with pictures by Dosso, Bellini and Titian. In his *Orlando Furioso*, Ariosto, court poet of Alfonso, places Dosso, who was court painter at that time, on a level with Mantegna, Leonardo, Bellini, Michelangelo and Raphael. The influence of Ariosto's poem can be detected in the present picture. The various beasts recall Pisanello's animal sketches, and the greyhound seems to be based on Dürer's engraving of Saint Eustace. Collections: William Graham, Robert H. and Evelyn Benson, London. *Kress Collection*, 1939.

JACOPO TINTORETTO · Venetian 1518-1594

Christ at the Sea of Galilee

The prodigious and superhuman in his genius shocks ordinary or placid souls. In truth, no such man has been seen before or since; he is as unique as Michelangelo, Rubens, and Titian. You may call him extravagant, hotheaded, an improviser; you may complain of the darkness of his colors, the contortion of his figures, the disorder of his groups, the hastiness of his brush, the strain and the mannerism which sometimes debase the originality of his style; you may accuse him of the defects of his qualities — that I will permit — but never has there been such a fiery furnace, so burning, so overflowing with outbursts and sputtering of flames, with such soaring of sparks, such sudden and manifold flashes of lighting, such a continuous blazing of unexpected smoke and lights.

I really do not know how to speak of him; I cannot describe his paintings, they are too vast and there are too many of them. It is the inner impetus of his spirit that one must describe; it seems to me that one discovers in him a unique condition, a lightning stroke of inspiration. That is a strong statement, but it corresponds to precise facts, that one can cite. In certain extreme moments, confronted by a great danger, a sudden shock, a man will see distinctly in a flash, with terrible intensity, years of his life, complete landscapes and scenes, sometimes a fragment of an imagined world: the memories of those who have been suffocated, the accounts of people who have narrowly escaped drowning, the confessions of would-be suicides and of opium smokers, and the Indian Puranas all testify to this. The active power of the mind suddenly increased tenfold, a hundredfold, makes the spirit live in this epitome of a moment, more than all the rest of its life. In truth, the result of such a sublime hallucination is usually prostration and illness; but when a temperament is strong enough to bear this electric shock without breaking down, a man like Luther, Saint Ignatius, Saint Paul or any of the great visionaries, will accomplish works that are beyond human capability. Such are the outbursts of creative imagination in the great artists; with fewer counterbalances they were as strong in Tintoretto as in the greatest masters. If one has properly understood the effect of this involuntary and extraordinary state on his tragic nature, and on his color sense, the rest follows from it. . . .

In comparison with him, all painters merely imitate each other. One is always surprised by his pictures; one wonders where he found all this, in what unknown world, fantastic and yet real.

HIPPOLYTE TAINE
Voyage en Italie (1866)

There is no simpler pleasure than looking at a fine Titian, unless it be looking at a fine Tintoret.

HENRY JAMES
Italian Hours (1909)

Canvas. Height 46⅛ in.; width 66½ in. (1.17 x 1.69). Painted c. 1562. Probably of the same period as the three paintings commissioned in 1562 for the Scuola di San Marco, now divided between the Accademia, Venice, and the Brera, Milan. In this picture, one of the most remarkable early seascapes in the history of art, Tintoretto anticipates the style of El Greco. The subject follows faithfully the scene described in John, XXI. Collections: Count J. Galotti; Arthur Sachs, New York. *Kress Collection*, 1939.

EL GRECO · SPANISH 1541-1614

The Virgin with Santa Inés and Santa Tecla

There was in him to my mind a temper that exactly suited the spirit that he found prevalent to some extent in Venice, and at its height in Rome. So he became the greatest of baroque painters. Looking at the whole series of his pictures I seem to see his interest in decoration for decoration's sake grow in intensity. His contemporaries thought that he painted in an increasingly fantastic manner because he went mad. I do not believe it. More recently it has been suggested that he suffered from astigmatism and it has been said that if you put on the right glasses his vertiginous figures would assume normal proportions. I do not believe it. Their immense elongation, which, I may remind the reader, he will find also in many of Tintoretto's pictures, seems to me a natural development of treating the human form as decoration. Because El Greco was aiming at this and nothing else I think he grew more and more indifferent to fact.... If he were alive to-day I imagine he would paint pictures as abstract as the later work of Bracque, Picasso and Fernand Léger. And it may be that the interest in formal design of the present day is due to the same causes as produced baroque art in the sixteenth century. Now too we are spiritually at sixes and sevens. Afraid of the sublime, we take refuge in the multiplication table....

But of course there is more in El Greco than the fantastic patterns he devised, his grace and distinction, the elegance of his gestures and his dramatic intensity, seldom falling into theatricalism, with which as I take it he satisfied the sardonic, ironic, sumptuous, sinister side of his nature.... Then there is his colour. This, I think, was the second of the two methods by which he strove to release his spirit from its burden; and it is his colour that makes him so wonderful an artist. A painter thinks with his brushes. Such thoughts as he has that can be put into words are for the most part commonplace. Why artists are often incomprehensible to other people is that they express their profoundest feelings in a language of their own. I think El Greco put the most serious emotion of his strange, perhaps inexplicable personality into the colours that he set down on canvas. However he acquired his palette, he gave it an intensity, a significance, which were his own. Colour was his complete and unique experience. They are not so far wrong who see in him a mystic, though I cannot help thinking that to look upon him as a religious mystic is superficial. If mysticism is that state that renders you conscious of depths of truth unknown to the intellect, revealing like "glimpses of forgotten dreams" a greater significance in life and union with some larger reality, then I think you can hardly fail to find it in El Greco's painting. I seem to see as great a mystic rapture in the painting of the right side of the body of Christ in the Crucifixion in the Louvre as in any of the experiences of Santa Teresa.

W. SOMERSET MAUGHAM
Don Fernando (1935)

Canvas. Height 76⅛ in.; width 40½ in. (1.93 x 1.03). Inscribed with the Greek initials of El Greco's name on the forehead of the lion. The painting was begun in 1597, according to the records of the lawsuit brought by the donors, who considered El Greco's charges exorbitant, and was completed in 1599. It was placed in the Chapel of San José in Toledo, where it formed a companion picture to the Saint Martin and the Beggar now in the National Gallery of Art, Widener Collection. Collections: The Chapel of San José, Toledo. *Widener Collection*, 1942.

VELAZQUEZ · Spanish 1599-1660

Pope Innocent X

Everything is done at the first stroke; no glazes, no overloaded colors, no professional tricks. The brush, freely playing in the thick pigments, where the trace of each hair is still visible, writes the forms, defines the muscles, identifies the setting, distributes light and shadow with sincerity and clarity and, at the same time, incomparable breadth. Never did a richer palette charm the eye. However, the general tone remains grave, for Velázquez does not employ colors which are in themselves brilliant. It is not by the use of blues, reds, greens and vivid yellows that he achieves that intense and luminous effect, that warm atmosphere which bathes his figures, but rather by broken tones, by skilful opposition of gradations, by an instinctive feeling for the color proper to objects. In this respect he is an unrivaled master. The Venetians and the Flemings do not have that restrained splendor, tranquil and profound, suggesting the luxury of houses which have enjoyed wealth for many generations.

However, Velázquez was realistic, like the art of his age, but how superior! He painted only from life, and having left the school of the frenzied Herrera, the Elder, to enter that of Pacheco, he would paint gourds, vegetables, game, fish and similar subjects, for practice.

The young master did not think these studies beneath his dignity. He brought to them that sovereign simplicity and that grandiose breadth which are the essence of his style, scorning all useless detail. Treated thus, these fruits might have been posed upon a golden platter on a royal sideboard; these viands, of epic import, might have figured at the Marriage at Cana. — Velázquez does not seek out beauty as did the great Italian artists, nor does he pursue ideal ugliness as do the realists of our age. He accepts nature as it is, freely, and reproduces it in its absolute truth, with a life, an illusion, and a miraculous power, so that whether beautiful, trivial, or ugly, it is always enhanced by the character and effect he bestows on it. Like the sun, which impartially sheds its light on all objects, converting a heap of straw into a mound of gold, a drop of water into a diamond, and a rag into a cloak of purple, Velázquez sheds his radiant color over all things, and without changing them gives them an inestimable value. — Touched by this brush, as by a fairy wand, ugliness becomes beauty; a deformed dwarf with a snub nose and flat wizened face delights the beholder more than a Venus or an Apollo. When Velázquez is confronted by beauty, how magnificently he expresses it, without witless flattery, preserving its bloom, its velvety quality, its grace, its charm, and augmenting it with a mysterious attraction, with a delicate and supreme strength! Have perfection pose for him, and he will paint it with a noble ease and not be overcome by it. Nothing that exists could baffle his brush.

Théophile Gautier
Tableaux à la plume (1880)

Canvas. Height 19¼ in.; width 16½ in. (0.49 x 0.42). Painted 1649-50. According to Beruete (*The School of Madrid*) this is a preliminary study from life for the celebrated portrait in the Doria Collection, Rome. It has an immediacy and an uncompromising realism afterwards generalized in the larger work. Collections: Acquired from the Walpole Collection, Houghton Hall, Norfolk, England, in 1779 for the Hermitage Gallery, Leningrad, by Catherine the Great. *Mellon Collection, 1937.*

MURILLO · SPANISH 1617-1682

A Girl and Her Duenna

He was an artist of feminine and receptive temperament, a realist indeed, but with no virile force, inapt to express the vigorous dramatic qualities which most natively find expression in Spanish art. But his hand was highly accomplished and his taste showed a finer sensibility than is common in Spain; he was sensitive to beauty, especially to the idyllic beauty of homely landscape scenes (though he was here largely a follower of Bassano), and to the plebeian charm of the Spanish peasant. His quick eye and ready hand were forced to adapt themselves to the needs of a city in which beauty was dedicated almost altogether to the service of religion. That circumstance, though it led to the production of pictures which made Murillo's fame, has yet been unfortunate for his reputation in the highest sense. Of all Spanish painters, Murillo alone, the genuine child of Andalusia, may be said to represent the spirit of what we term the "South." For that very reason, perhaps, he was not so typically and essentially Spanish as Ribera was. He was without the Spanish dramatic aptitude, without the sincerity of intense religious feeling. Murillo's famous Virgins in the clouds, after the manner of Ribera's great Salamanca "Conception," however delicious the glowing haze in which they live, are nearly always pretty peasant girls, posing in beautiful robes that do not belong to them, and simulating ecstatic emotions they have never felt. His other religious pictures are similarly gracious and charming, similarly unconvincing. When we can forget that we are looking at a religious picture, or when the painter was free to devote himself to frankly secular subjects, we can better enjoy the qualities of his art. It is true that his beggar-boys are just as deliberately and self-consciously picturesque as his saints are deliberately and self-consciously holy. Still, no other Spanish painter has so agreeably seized the peasant life of Spain, or rather of Andalusia, at the points where it fell in harmoniously with his own pretty mannerisms; in this field, indeed, he sometimes seems both sensitive and sincere, able to present life for what it is worth. Even the absence of dramatic instinct helped him here. His love of beauty and refinement, especially when manifested in a plebeian shape, his idyllic feeling for the beauty of pastoral repose in a patriarchal age . . . . his softly bright and luminous colouring, his facile skill in realistic detail — all these things must make Murillo a fascinating and peculiar figure in Spanish painting, though they cannot enable us to place him beside Velazquez and Ribera.

HAVELOCK ELLIS
The Soul of Spain (1908)

Canvas. Height 49¼ in.; width 41½ in. (1.25 x 1.05). Painted about 1665-1675. Traditionally known as Las Gallegas, the Galicians, because the painting is said to portray two notorious courtesans of Seville, sisters who had come to the city from the province of Galicia. A slightly smaller repetition of this painting was in the Munro-Ferguson Collection at Novar, Rossshire. Collections: The Duke of Almodovar, Madrid; Lord Heytesbury, Wiltshire. *Widener Collection,* 1942.

HANS HOLBEIN, THE YOUNGER · German 1497-1543

Edward VI as Prince of Wales

There are two ways of conceiving the portrait — the historic and the romantic. The first is to render faithfully, severely, scrupulously, the contour and the modeling of the subject. This does not exclude idealization, which for the learned naturalists will consist of choosing the most characteristic attitude, that which best expresses the habits of the spirit; and furthermore, in knowing how to give each important detail a reasonable emphasis, placing in the light all that is naturally salient, accentuated and prominent, and neglecting or blending in the whole all that is insignificant, or what is the result of an accidental diminution in significance.

The second method, the one peculiar to colorists, is to make of the portrait a picture, a poem with its accessories, full of space and reverie. Here the art is more difficult, because it is more ambitious. One must know how to bathe a head in the soft vapors of a torrid atmosphere, or to make it emerge from the depths of the twilight. Here the imagination plays a greater part, and yet, just as fiction often surpasses history in truth, a subject may be more clearly defined by the facile and flowing brush of the colorist than by the pencil of the draftsman. Portraiture, apparently such a modest branch of the arts, demands immense intelligence. Unquestionably the artist must be very faithful to his model, but his insight must equal his fidelity. When I see a good portrait I think of all the efforts of the artist, who has had first to see what was evident, but also to divine what was hidden. I was just now comparing him to a historian; I might also compare him to a comedian, who of necessity feigns all characters and dons every kind of costume. Nothing, if one examines the matter well, is inconsequential in a portrait. The gesture, the grimace, the garment, even the setting — all must play a part in representing a *character*. Among great painters and excellent painters, David, both when he was but another artist of the eighteenth century and after he had become the leader of a school, and Holbein in all his portraits, tried to express with restraint but with intensity the character they undertook to paint. Others sought to do even more, or to do otherwise. Reynolds and Gérard supplied the romantic touch, always in accord with the nature of the personage; hence a stormy and tormented sky, light and airy backgrounds, poetic furnishings, a languishing attitude, an adventurous bearing. This is a dangerous procedure, which, while not to be condemned, nevertheless calls for genius. Finally, whatever the means most obviously used by the artist, whether that artist be Holbein, David, Velázquez or Lawrence, a good portrait appears to me always as a dramatized biography, or better as the human drama inherent in every man.

Charles Baudelaire
Salon de 1859
Revue Française (1859)

Wood. Height 22½ in.; width 17⅜ in. (0.57 x 0.44). Painted 1538, soon after Holbein's second arrival in England, and generally accepted as the portrait of the Prince recorded as presented to the King on New Year's Day, 1539. The drawing which doubtless served as the study for this panel is in Windsor Castle (Woltmann, *Holbein*). The Latin inscription is a *consilium* addressed to the Prince by Sir Richard Morison. ambassador and close friend of Henry VIII: *Little one, emulate thy father; become heir to the virtue of him whose peer the world does not possess. Heaven and earth could hardly produce a son to surpass in glory such a father. Do but match in full thy parent's deeds and men can ask no more. Shouldst thou surpass him, thou hast outstript all kings the world revered in ages past.* Collections: From the English Royal Collection the portrait passed in the eighteenth century to the Royal and Ducal Hanoverian Collections. In 1893 it was deposited in the Provincial Museum, Hanover. *Mellon Collection,* 1937.

PARVVLE PATRISSA, PATRIÆ VIRTVTIS ET HÆRES
    ESTO, NIHIL MAIVS MAXIMVS ORBIS HABET.
GNATVM VIX POSSVNT COELVM ET NATVRA DEDISSE,
    HVIVS QVEM PATRIS, VICTVS HONORET HONOS.
ÆQVATO TANTVM, TANTI TV FACTA PARENTIS,
    VOTA HOMINVM, VIX QVO PROGREDIANTVR, HABENT
VINCITO, VICISTI. QVOT REGES PRISCVS ADORAT
    ORBIS, NEC TE QVI VINCERE POSSIT, ERIT. Ricard Morysyn Cer.

JAN VAN EYCK · FLEMISH 1380/1400-1441

The Annunciation

Another work of the master, which lends itself particularly to the analysis of endless detail, is the "Annunciation". . . . If the triptych of which this picture formed the right wing ever existed as a whole, it must have been a superb creation. Van Eyck here developed all the virtuosity of a master conscious of his power to overcome all difficulties. Of all his works it is the most hieratic and, at the same time, the most refined. He followed the iconographic rules of the past in using as a background for the apparition of the angel the ample space of a church and not the intimacy of a bed-chamber, as he did in the altar-piece of the Lamb, where the scene is full of grace and tenderness. Here, on the contrary, the angel salutes Mary by a ceremonious bow; he is not represented with a spray of lilies and a narrow diadem; he carries a sceptre and a rich crown, and about his lips there is the stiff smile of the sculpture of Ægina. The splendour of the colours, the glitter of the pearls, the gold and the precious stones, surpass those of all the other angelic figures painted by Van Eyck. His coat is green and gold, his mantle of brocade is red and gold, his wings are covered with peacock feathers. The book of the Virgin and the cushion before her are executed with pains-taking and minute care. In the church there is a profusion of anecdotal details. The tiles of the pavement are ornamented with the signs of the zodiac and scenes from the lives of Samson and of David. The wall of the apse is decorated with the figures of Isaac and of Jacob in the medallions between the arches, and that of Christ on the celestial globe between two seraphim in a window, besides other mural paintings representing the finding of the child Moses and the giving of the tables of the Law, all explained by legible inscriptions. Only the decoration of the wooden ceiling, though still discernible, remains indistinct.

This time unity and harmony are not lost in the accumulation of details. The twilight of the lofty edifice envelops all with mysterious shade, so that the eye can only with difficulty distinguish the anecdotal details.

It is the privilege of the painter that he can give the rein to his craving for endless elaboration of details (perhaps one ought to say, that he can comply with the most impossible demands of an ignorant donor) without sacrificing the general effect. The sight of this multitude of details fatigues us no more than the sight of reality itself. We only notice them if our attention has been directed to them, and we soon lose sight of them, so that they serve only to heighten effects of colouring or perspective.

JOHAN HUIZINGA
The Waning of the Middle Ages (1924)

Transferred from wood to canvas. Height 36¾ in.; width 14½ in. (0.93 x 0.37). Probably one of the wings of a lost triptych. Painted in the same period as the triptych in Dresden and the Ghent altarpiece, which was finished in 1432. Scenes of the Old Testament represented on the graffito floor and on the wall foretell the events of the New Testament, while the Romanesque architecture symbolizes the era before the incarnation of Christ. The building cannot be identified with an existing Flemish church, but the wall paintings and capitals reproduce with meticulous accuracy the late Romanesque style of Maastricht and Tournay. Such archæological exactness is unique for an artist of this period. Collections: Said to have come from a church in Dijon, the painting was sold by Charles J. Nieuwenhuys of Brussels to William II, King of the Netherlands, in 1819. From his estate it was purchased by Czar Nicholas I in 1850, for the Hermitage Gallery, Leningrad. *Mellon Collection*, 1937.

ROGIER VAN DER WEYDEN · Flemish 1399/1400-1464

Portrait of a Lady

The Flemish primitives were the greatest painters in the world, Durtal said to himself, and this Roger van der Weyden, or as others call him, this Roger de La Pasture, overwhelmed by the fame of Van Eyck and of Memling, even as, at a later date, were Gerard David, Hugo van der Goes, Justus of Ghent, Dirk Bouts, is, in my opinion, superior to all of them.

J.-K. Huysmans
La Cathédrale (1898)

The men and women out of that past are as children to us with our mechanical inventions, but we are in the same stature to them, dwarfed before their giant eminence where the poetry of the senses is concerned. Therefore, not only is antiquity sad because it is so old, ageing a little even as we think of it, but, also, its living force was something that we have missed. The massed effects and properties of those expired centuries give the illusion of something existing parallel to, but divided from, ourselves. It is the very world in which we want to live, lying near to us, but impossible to touch, or be in communion with; separated from us, so it seems, by some barrier whose nature we cannot either define, or overcome. Thus, its whole total is, in a sense, contemporary with us, and yet by no effort can we break into its area, and it is kept away from us by some infrangible rule that neither body nor mind can contradict.

It is easy enough to personify this loss. The casting for its characters need go no further than .... a sisterhood of Ophelias, for this nunnery encloses a race, all alike, and of one pattern. The thin distension and elaboration of their form is as though they were only to be seen through a film of water, which has combed back their long, flat hair with its weedy fingers and pressed their whole symmetry into its own limpid convenience. The fine hands, pale as milk and tapering to the nail-points, seem to have been rubbed with honey from the dropped flowers floating on the stream, or from the lilies that live of their own volition upon the waters. ... As to the mind hidden behind this chastity and its defences, the very extent of its shortcomings is an absorbing mystery, which becomes still stranger on investigation. Then, this veil between ourselves and the past is lifted a little, but only to that point of comprehension which might be reached if speech was only possible with the eyes and any understanding of the lips was still forbidden. But no further point than this is ever arrived at, and, here, only half-way into words, this communion is interrupted and can never be improved into permanence.

The body of this beautiful and strange mystery lies so close to us that we can feel the warm emanation coming from it, but our eyes, the only contact we have with it, never tell us of any change, though such lover's blindness is unwarranted and the gradual, slow decay of this ideal should be visible even to ourselves.

Sacheverell Sitwell
The Gothick North (1930)

Wood. Height 14½ in.; width 10¾ in. (0.37 x 0.27). Painted c. 1455. The sitter has not been definitely identified, although the name of Marie de Valengin, illegitimate daughter of Philip the Good of Burgundy, has been suggested. Collections: Ducal House of Anhalt-Dessau, Gotisches Haus, Wörlitz. *Mellon Collection*, 1937.

GERARD DAVID · Flemish c. 1460-1523

The Rest on the Flight into Egypt

He was old-fashioned, but genuinely so. It was not a pose. He was constitutionally religious. One might imagine him at home with the Brethren of the Common Life or any of the mystic fellowships whose days of vitality were coming to an end when David was born. The atmosphere of his pictures is like that of *The Imitation of Christ*. David was the only Northern artist who ever painted a St. Francis at all acceptably. The little wing picture of the Stigmatization is almost credible. The painter felt and rendered something of the ecstasy of the Saint. In face and figure he is wholly wrapt up in his vision. The contrast between him and the unfelt John the Baptist on the pendant is remarkable. The latter is a mere emblem, emotionless, meaningless. The former is intoxicated with God. David's nature seems to me to have been a deeper one than Memling's. There is much in common in the spirit of their art, but Memling, for all his dexterous and pleasant handling, is more superficial, more like a man who adapts himself, easily and naturally enough, yet still adapts himself, to the taste of the little society for whom he worked. David needed no adaptation. He painted what and how he really liked to paint. . . .

With his conservative religious tendencies, David had no temptation to devise original treatments for the round of sacred subjects he had to paint. To borrow was but to follow the good old tradition. What David did not and could not have borrowed was the reverential mood that governed his hand. Forms and details he could pick up here and there as he saw what pleased him, but his art was not in the forms. Its vitality was deep within himself. Alike in the *naïveté* of his earliest works and the complete harmony and expressiveness of the later, the spirit is the same. A single pure and simple character is behind them all. It follows that the handiwork of the man is of a piece with his nature. We need not look to him for technical innovations nor fear to be put off with a slipshod technique. There is nothing cheap about David's art. If half a hundred or more of his pictures have survived the misuse of men through half a thousand years it is because their maker was a thoroughly sound and conscientious craftsman. His methods were those of the Van Eycks, and of the best of their successors throughout the fifteenth century. All that was personal to him about them was his selection and combination of colours. His best pictures have a richness all their own.

SIR MARTIN CONWAY
The Van Eycks and Their Followers (1921)

Wood. Height 17⅜ in.; width 17⅜ in. (0.44 x 0.44). Painted after 1509. The Christ Child with the grapes, a eucharistic symbol, is closely related to David's picture in the Museum at Rouen, painted in 1509 for the Carmelites of Sion. The figure of St. Joseph beating chestnuts from a tree is derived from calendar illustrations of Flemish illuminated manuscripts. The picture must have been extremely popular, as evidenced by the many existing contemporary copies, and altered School replicas such as that by Ysenbrandt in the Philip Lehman Collection, New York. The motif of the wicker basket of the Virgin recurs throughout the sixteenth century, for instance, in Patinir and Jan Brueghel. Collections: Rodolphe Kann, Paris; J. Pierpont Morgan, New York. *Mellon Collection*, 1937.

PETER PAUL RUBENS · FLEMISH 1577-1640

Isabella Brant

Rubens has, more than all other painters, made the way to colouring easy and clear. . . . I am sensible, that many differ from my opinion of this great man's works, and that of a very considerable number of painters, and curious men, who have with all their might opposed my opinion, when I brought to light, if I may so say, the merit of this great man, who before was considered as a painter but little above the common level: of these people, I say, some yet remain, who without distinguishing the different parts of painting, especially colouring, of which we are now speaking, value nothing but the *Roman* manner, the taste of *Poussin,* and the school of the *Carracchis.*

They object, among other things, that *Rubens's* works appear to have little truth, on a near examination; that the colours and lights are loaded; and that, in the main, they are but a daubing, and very different from what we commonly observe in nature.

It is true, they are but a daubing; but it were to be wished, that the pictures that are now painted, were all daubed in the same manner. Painting, in general, is but daubing; its essence lies in deceiving, and the greatest deceiver is the best painter. Nature in herself is unseemly, and he who copies her servilely, and without artifice, will always produce something poor, and of a mean taste. What is called *load,* in colours and lights, can only proceed from a profound knowledge in the values of colours, and from an admirable industry, which makes the painted objects appear more true, if I may say so, than the real ones. In this sense it may be asserted, that, in *Rubens's* pieces, art is above nature, and nature only a copy of that great master's works. And of what import is it, after all, if things, on examination, be not perfectly just? If they appear so, they answer the end of painting, which is not so much to convince the understanding, as to deceive the eye.

This artifice will always appear wonderful in great works; for when the picture is distanced according to its bigness, it is this artifice which supports the character, both of the particular objects, and of the whole together; but without it the work, in proportion as we remove from it, will appear to remove from truth, and look as insipid as an ordinary painting. 'Tis in such great works, that *Rubens* is observed to have so happily succeeded in this learned and apparent load, by those especially who are capable of giving attention, and of examining it; for, to others, nothing can be a greater mystery.

ROGER DE PILES
Cours de peinture par principes (1708)

Canvas. Height 60¼ in.; width 47¼ in. (1.53 x 1.20). The critics who believe this painting to be by Rubens date it between 1623 and 1626. In the latter year Isabella died, and in the present picture the face of the sitter seems drawn, as though it were pinched and worn by illness. The critics who believe the portrait to be by Van Dyck date it prior to his Italian journey in 1621, and do not attempt to identify the sitter. The ornamental gateway in the background formed a part of the garden of Rubens' palace in Antwerp. Collections: Purchased from the Crozat Collection, Paris, by Catherine the Great of Russia for the Hermitage Gallery, Leningrad. *Mellon Collection,* 1937.

SIR ANTHONY VAN DYCK · FLEMISH 1599-1641

Marchesa Elena Grimaldi, Wife of Marchese Nicola Cattaneo

This is what I should imagine a portrait of Van Dyck to be like, in a rough sketch, with unblended crayon strokes.

A young prince of royal blood, with everything in his favour — beauty, elegance, magnificent parts, precocious genius, unique education, and with all the chance happenings of fortunate birth before him; petted by his master, already himself a master among his schoolfellows, admired everywhere, invited everywhere, welcomed everywhere, abroad even more than in his own country; the equal of the greatest lords, the favourite and friend of kings; entering thus, at one stroke, into possession of all the most desirable things of this earth — talent, fame, honours, luxury, love, adventure; ever young, even in his mature years; never wise, even in his last years; a libertine, a gambler, greedy, prodigal, wasteful, playing the devil, and as they would have said in his time, selling his soul to the devil for guineas, and then throwing them away open-handed, for horses, display, feasts, ruinous gallantries; enamoured of his art in the highest degree, yet sacrificing it to less noble passions, to less faithful amours, to less fortunate attachments; charming, of strong race, of slender, elegant stature, as happens in the second remove of great races; of a constitution already less virile, rather delicate, in fact; with the air of a Don Juan rather than of a hero, with a tinge of melancholy and an undertone of sadness underlying all the gaiety of his life, the impressionableness of a heart easily smitten, and that something of disillusionment proper to those whose hearts are too easily smitten; a nature inflammable rather than burning; at bottom, more sensuality than real fire, less transport than unrestraint; less capable of grasping things than of allowing himself to be seized by them and of abandoning himself to them; a man delightful in his own attractiveness and sensible to all other attractiveness, devoured by that which is most consuming in this world — the muse and women; having abused everything — his charms, his health, his dignity, his talent; overwhelmed with needs, worn out by pleasure, drained of resources; an insatiable being who ended, they say, by keeping low company with Italian rascals and by seeking surreptitiously the Philosopher's Stone; an adventurer at his last resources, who married, by command so to speak, a charming, high-born lady, at a time when he had little to offer her — not much strength, not much money, no longer any great charm nor very certain life; the wreck of a man who, up to his last hour, had the good fortune — the most extraordinary of all — to keep his greatness when he painted; in short, a scamp, adored, decried, slandered later on, at bottom better than he was reputed to be, and a man who gained pardon for all his faults by a supreme gift, one of the forms of genius — grace; to put it plainly — a Prince of Wales dying as soon as the throne was empty, and who was not to reign.

EUGÈNE FROMENTIN
Les Maîtres d'autrefois (1876)

Canvas. Height 97 in.; width 68 in. (2.46 x 1.73). Painted c. 1623. This portrait and the portraits of the two children of the Marchesa, also in the National Gallery of Art, Widener Collection, are among the supreme achievements of Van Dyck's Italian period. Collections: Cattaneo Palace, Genoa. *Widener Collection,* 1942.

SIR ANTHONY VAN DYCK · FLEMISH 1599-1641

Philip, Lord Wharton

The case of Van Dyck deserves a special analysis. Although it touches upon the philosophy of portrait-painting, it is still directly relevant to our thesis. It may well be asked whether this Prince of Wales of painting (to retain the title given him by Fromentin) did not in large measure contribute to the *creation* of a social environment, thus reversing the terms of a commonly accepted proposition. Van Dyck lives in an England that is still crude and violent, still torn by revolutions, still given over to the pleasures of the instinct, and still maintaining beneath the thin varnish of court life the appetites of "Merry England." He paints its heroes and heroines with his own native distinction, even when his models are such plain and worthy folk as fat Endymion Porter. He discovers and discloses in pretty girls and in adventurers of worldly gallantry that dashing look, that cavalier bravery, and even that romantic melancholy which, first of all, lie wholly within himself, and with which, as with some charming seal, he laid his mark upon his poets and captains. Here it is that the brilliant flower of his painting comes into play — that precious material, fine and fluid, those shimmering, musical notes which compose one of the most delicate luxuries ever made for our eyes. Here he holds up to English snobbishness the mirror in which henceforth, for generations, through all the changes of taste, it complacently views itself. Even today those who sit for a fashionable painter unconsciously wish to resemble the portraits of long ago, and behind these admirable figures of modern English gentlemen one seems to divine the invisible presence of their secret arbiter — Van Dyck himself.

HENRI FOCILLON
Vie des formes (1934)

Canvas. Height 52¾ in.; width 42 in. (1.34 x 1.07). The marriage of the young Lord Wharton, in 1632, may have been the occasion for the portrait. Collections: Lord Wharton, Winchendon, Buckinghamshire; Robert Walpole, Houghton Hall, Norfolk, England; Hermitage Gallery, Leningrad. *Mellon Collection,* 1937.

FRANS HALS · DUTCH c. 1580-1666

Balthasar Coymans

Drop the catalogue and use your own eyes. The first impression is profound; not that Hals was profound in the sense of Rembrandt's profundity, but because of the almost terrifying vitality of these portraits. Prosaic men and women, great trenchermen, devourers of huge pasties, mowers down of wine-bottles and beer-tankards, they live with such vitality on the canvases of Hals that you instinctively lower your voice. The paint-imprisoned ghosts of these jolly officers, sharpshooters, regents, and shrewd-looking old women regents are not so disquieting as Rembrandt's misty evocations. They touch hands with you across the centuries, and finally you wonder why they don't step out the frame and greet you. Withal, no trace of literalism, of obvious contours or tricky effects. Honest, solid paint, but handled by the greatest master of the brush that ever lived — save Velasquez. How thin and unsubstantial modern painting is if compared to this magician, how even his greatest followers, Manet and Sargent, seem incomplete. Manet, with his abridgments, his suppressions, his elliptical handling, never had the smiling confidence of Hals in facing a problem. The Frenchman is more subtle, also more evasive; and there is no hint in him of the trite statement of a fact that we encounter in Bartholomew Van der Helst — himself a great painter. Hals had not the poetic vision of Rembrandt, but he possessed a more dexterous hand, a keener eye. Judged according to the rubric of sheer paint, sheer brush-work, not Rubens, not Van Dyck, was such a virtuoso. Despite his almost incredible swiftness of execution, Hals got closer to the surfaces of what is called "actual" life than any of the masters with the exception of the supreme Spaniard. . . .

What a colourist! What nuances he produces on a restrained key-board! The tones modulate, their juxtaposition causes no harsh discords. The velvet black, silvery grays, whites that are mellow without pastiness, and the reds and yellows do not flare out like scarlet trumpets; an aristocratic palette. Really you begin to realise that what you formerly considered grandfather tales are the truth. The great painters have been and are not with us to-day. It is not a consoling pill to swallow for apostles of "modernity." Hals is more modern than Sargent. . . .

Hals shows us not the magic of life but the normal life of daylight in which move with dignity men and women undismayed by the mysteries that hem them about. He has a daylight soul, a sane if not poetic soul, and few painters before him so celebrated the bravery of appearances, the beauty of the real.

JAMES HUNEKER
Promenades of an Impressionist (1910)

Canvas. Height 30¼ in.; width 25 in. (0.77 x 0.64). By means of the coat of arms, van Lennep (*Burlington Magazine,* 1908) has verified the traditional connection of this portrait with the Coymans or Koeymans family. The date indicates that the sitter must be Balthasar (1618-1690), Lord of Streefkerk and Nieuw Lekkerland and Alderman of Haarlem. Collections: Coymans Family, Haarlem; Rodolphe Kann, Paris; Mrs. Collis P. Huntington Collection, New York. *Mellon Collection,* 1937.

REMBRANDT · DUTCH 1606-1669

Self-Portrait

As we know, the sensual and the aesthetic do not necessarily coincide, though they may overlap. Rembrandt made no attempt to squeeze his subjects into the mould of Beauty as prescribed by an alien tradition: he took people as he found them and he found them good. Only in his younger days, amused by exotic display, he dressed himself and his models up in pseudo-oriental finery; but maturing, discarded this nonsense in favour of the fashions of his time, with always, it is true, a predilection for the de-moded and well-worn habiliments of the very poor.

Later a plain chemise, a blanket or a few rags were all he needed, his ward-robe being empty (if he had one). But the forms they dissembled were no less alive, and for him life was all that mattered. The brooding femininity of Hendrickje calls for no bedizenment; her eyes provide adequate jewelry as they gaze out of the shadows and convey a secret which her mouth re-iterates, silent but smiling within the golden penumbra of her master's vision.

Blackmailed, ruined, ostracized and deserted by his rich patrons, the artist removes to the Jewish quarter and there with his partner and his Bible continues to paint with ever increasing power. Does Jan Six venture to visit his old friend? No. What of his numerous pupils, above all Nicolas Maes? We are not told. And thus in gloom and mystery, illuminated solely by the transposed sunlight of his genius, the greatest Dutchman dies, content, we must think, that like Poussin he had "neglected nothing."

AUGUSTUS JOHN
A Note on Rembrandt
The Burlington Magazine (1942)

Canvas. Height 33¼ in.; width 26 in. (0.84 x 0.66). Signed, and dated 1659. Starting with the self-portrait of 1652, Rembrandt shows an increased interest in psychological interpretation. His self-portraits from this date until his death constitute an almost unbroken record of his life. The picture on the right is, in pose and costume, most closely related to the self-portrait dated 1659 in the Collection of the Earl of Ellesmere, Bridgewater House, London. Two other self-portraits (Museum, Aix-en-Provence, and National Gallery, London) also show Rembrandt at about the age of fifty-three. Collections: Duke of Buccleuch, Scotland. *Mellon Collection, 1937.*

REMBRANDT · DUTCH 1606-1669

The Mill

Rembrandt's "Mill" is a picture wholly made by chiaroscuro; the last ray of light just gleams on the upper sail of the mill, and all other details are lost in large and simple masses of shade. Chiaroscuro is the great feature that characterizes his art, and was carried farther by him than by any other painter, not excepting Correggio. But if its effects are somewhat exaggerated by Rembrandt, he is always so impressive, that we can no more find fault with his style than we can with the giant forms of Michael Angelo. Succeeding painters have sometimes, in their admiration of "The Mill," forgotten that Rembrandt chose the twilight to second his wishes, and have fancied that to obtain equal breadth, they must leave out the details of nature in broad daylight; this is the danger of mistaken imitation.

JOHN CONSTABLE
Lectures on Landscape Painting (1836)

As the keen stimulus derived from good figure painting may be compared to the excitement of an active intellectual life, so the effect of landscape upon us may be compared to that of a country holiday. The periods in which contemplation takes the place of action may not, from a material point of view, have been the most important in our lives; they may have included no serious crisis of our fortunes, they may recall no decisive triumphs. Nevertheless, in after years it is to these times of repose that our minds revert most pleasurably and most definitely. The details of our troubles and our strivings are apt to become vague memories, until it seems as if the whole of our active existence had been one long uneasy dream, and our holidays the only moments in which we were awake to the reality of life.

Landscape, then, might be described as the pictorial interpretation of man's communion with nature, and its functions are, in their degree, analogous to those of that communion. The mission of landscape is thus to soothe the spirit rather than to excite it, to open out a prospect of quiet, of solitude, or of space. It can stimulate, too, but it stimulates by the indirect process of nature herself — by a gradual attraction rather than by any sudden shock or striking exhibition of force. It can exhilarate by movement, though the movement will not be the strong sweep of the passions, or the agitation of a troubled spirit, but the tonic ebb and flow of the fresh air of heaven. Landscape can also accomplish that purging of the emotions by pity and fear, which for more than two thousand years has been recognised as the function of all tragic art, though it does not do so by the heroic strife or godlike rest of those magnified images of our own humanity which have been the recognised puppets of all the great figure painters, great sculptors, and great poets. The tragic power of landscape lies in its command of the irresistible forces of nature — the storm, the cataract, or the angry sea — and those hardly less tremendous emblems of her repose, the mountains and the twilight.

C. J. HOLMES
Constable and His Influence on Landscape Painting (1902)

Canvas. Height 33⅞ in.; width 40⅛ in. (0.86 x 1.02). Painted about 1650, according to most authorities. The Mill has had a strong influence on English landscape painting. Turner admired it greatly, and the notes in his sketchbook show it was the basis of his conception of Rembrandt's handling of light. Charles Turner engraved it in his *Gems of Art*. Collections: Duc d'Orléans, Paris; Marquess of Lansdowne, Bowood Hall, Wiltshire, England. *Widener Collection*, 1942.

JAN VERMEER · Dutch 1632-1675

Young Girl with a Flute

Vermeer's most prodigious quality, surpassing even his instinct for physiognomy, is the quality of his light.

Vivid light effects are not very difficult to achieve by means of contrast with deep shadows. I, for one, am not too fond of Ribera's and Caravaggio's contrasts, those clashes between white and black that characterize the manner of the *tenebrosi* admired in Italy in the seventeenth century. The two great masters of light are, in my opinion, and for different reasons, Velázquez and Rembrandt. The latter controls the gradation of light down to the point of darkness and illumines even the darkness; the former pours out a full light without the opposition of shadows. Both are incomparable, Rembrandt especially for his interiors, Velázquez for his outdoor scenes, both — these naturalists! — nevertheless treat the effects of light poetically, and with an arbitrariness far removed from the natural effect. . . .

In Vermeer's work, the light is not at all artificial: it is precise and normal as in nature, such as a scrupulous physicist would wish it. The ray that enters at one side of the frame penetrates space to the other side. The light seems to come from the painting itself, and the ingenuous spectator might readily imagine that the daylight slips in between the canvas and the frame. Someone, visiting Monsieur Double, where *The Soldier and the Laughing Girl* was displayed on an easel, walked around behind the picture to see where this wonderful radiance at the open window came from. Consequently, black frames suit Vermeer's pictures very well.

Rembrandt's skin tones are golden, his shadows the color of chestnut. Vermeer's lights are silver, his shadows the color of pearls.

In Vermeer there is no black at all, no smearing or blurring. There is light everywhere, back of an armchair, a table or a harpsichord, as well as near the window. But each object has exactly the right half-lights, and mingles its reflections with the ambient rays. It is to this accuracy of light that Vermeer owes the harmony of his colors. In his pictures, as in nature, antipathetic colors such as yellow and blue, of which he is particularly fond, lose their dissonance. He combines tones that are extremely foreign to one another, passing from the tenderest minor key to the most exalted intensity. Brilliance, energy, subtlety, variety, the unexpected and the strange, the indescribable quality of rarity and of appeal — he has all these gifts of the bold colorists, for whom light is an inexhaustible magician.

W. Bürger (Thoré)
Van der Meer de Delft
Gazette des Beaux-Arts (1866)

Wood. Height 7⅞ in.; width 7 in. (0.20 x 0.18). Painted c. 1660. This painting is a pendant to The Girl with a Red Hat in the Mellon Collection, National Gallery of Art. In a sale on May 16, 1696 at Amsterdam, three works by Vermeer are listed as "Portraits in Antique Costume." It is possible that the Young Girl with a Flute and The Girl with a Red Hat were two of these items. Collections: Mahie van Boxtel en Liempde, 's Hertogenbosch, Holland; Jonkheer de Grez, Brussels; August Janssen, Amsterdam. *Widener Collection*, 1942.

JAN VERMEER · Dutch 1632-1675

Woman Weighing Gold

The artist seldom seems to intervene, to rearrange things, to explain what is taking place, what his models are feeling, or to make any personal comment. A young girl, her privacy unwittingly betrayed by a door left ajar, reveals life's even tenor. It is as though the painter were not there. And yet few paintings have an equal capacity for evoking reverie, that capacity one finds in certain Sienese or Umbrian Madonnas, who neither think nor act but remain immobile, not even smiling, with tireless intensity of gaze. An unhurried life, quiet pursuits, calm spirits, eternal gestures, the beauty of silence and of peace, as of still waters, the artlessness of the daylight, the enchantment of the innocent eye which imparts wonder to all it beholds — paintings which make one comprehend Flaubert's words: "It seems to me that the apogee of art (and the most difficult height to achieve) is not to evoke laughter or tears nor to arouse passion or rage but rather to do as nature does, that is to say, *to evoke dreams.*"

Finally one finds in Vermeer an individual poesy, an ineffable voluptuousness which is the result of his very manner of painting: you could not find a more homogeneous surface, a smoother or more luminous one, a surface which has the charm of fine porcelain, and which (along with his decorative sense) the artist may have inherited from the ceramists of his native land. In general, he composes everything, and without any apparent sacrifice, around a single pure tone, rose, yellow, frequently a blue that dominates the center of the picture, upon a woman's dress or bodice, and which radiates against the white background. No one else has been able to impart such a luminous quality to a single, usually rather cool color. It is this note which one remembers, and which sings in the memory, unique and unforgettable, despite the wealth of tones surrounding it, even though the author does not dim these tones in order to make a single point in the picture more vibrant. He uses chiaroscuro, but in a manner totally different from that of Rembrandt: he paints as the sun illuminates, without the least sacrifice of the simple truth (although he also has an inclination toward studied refinement and a subtle penchant for the bizarre, which is an added charm, as for example in the allegory of *The Triumph of Religion,* formerly in Amsterdam). And in his great picture in Vienna, *The Painter and His Model* (Czernin Collection), he is unquestionably the only master who rivals the poetry of Velázquez' *Las Meninas,* that is to say, the only one who has in some incomprehensible way combined in the representation of life so much actuality and so much mystery.

Louis Gillet
La Peinture en Europe au XVIIe siècle (1934)

Canvas. Height 16½ in.; width 14 in. (0.42 x 0.36). Painted c. 1654-1657. Few paintings by Vermeer have so complete a history as the present picture. It was sold in Amsterdam in 1696, and again in 1701. It was bought by Van den Bogaerde at the Nieuwhof sale at Amsterdam in 1777. In 1826 it appeared in Munich, at the sale of the possessions of the King of Bavaria, and was purchased by the Duc de Caraman, Paris. In 1830 it passed into the Collection of Casimir-Périer, London. It was sold at auction in 1848, and entered the Collection of the Comtesse de Ségur, where it remained until brought to America in 1911. *Widener Collection,* 1942.

PIETER DE HOOCH · Dutch 1629–c. 1683

A Dutch Courtyard

I venture to propose the probably rash idea that, if the Dutch painters avoid narrative subjects, of literary and dramatic significance, if they make use of anonymous actors supplemented by generalized landscapes, it is because they wish to represent not actions, not events, but moods. As the landscapes that I have just been describing give us a sense of space, so the intimate scenes of which I am now going to speak make us conscious of time. They are the reservoir of evanescent feelings. We do not merely glance at a painting by . . . . Vermeer, or Pieter de Hooch with condescending approval; we are immediately within it, we live there. We are entrapped. We are enclosed in it. We feel the form of it on us like a garment. We are saturated with its atmosphere, which we absorb through all our pores, through all our sensibilities, and, as it were, through the inlets of our very being. And, indeed, the dwelling where we are has a soul. It receives, separates and distributes the exterior ray, as does our own. It is completely filled with the stillness of the present moment. In it we witness the process that goes on within ourselves, by which outer reality is translated into light and shadow, the step-by-step motion of the daylight which rises and descends upon the wall that we present to it within our consciousness. The series of rooms and courts, the glimpse yonder of the garden through an open door, or of the sky through a transom, far from distracting us, gives us a more peaceful enjoyment of our seclusion and security. This is our reserved domain. As a sudden touch sets aglow in us a memory or an idea, as steadily increasing illumination models a figure and gives it volume, so the Dutch artist is expert in withholding and in using this mystic dowry that the passing hours pour out to him. . . . The waterlike transparency of windowpanes, the variations in the density of the air, the complex interaction of walls, and the reflections of reflections that are thrown back from one wall to the other, the checkered trellis-work that slants across a wall and that the fixed eye of a mirror records in reverse, the contrast in the midst of a room between the lighted and unlighted parts, between what has just been lighted up and that which is getting dark, the furnishings, heavy, dull-faced chests and glowing coppers, which give character to the whole — all this composes a kind of talisman, a kind of intimate formula or secret charm, and makes one understand how the people who live here cannot escape from this domestic paradise.

PAUL CLAUDEL
Introduction à la peinture hollandaise (1935)

Canvas. Height 26¾ in.; width 23⅛ in. (0.68 x 0.59). Painted c. 1656. Another version of this picture, lacking the cavalier holding the beer jug, belongs to the Ten Cate Collection, Almelo, Holland. Collections: C. S. Roos, Isaac van Eyck, Amsterdam; S. A. Koopman, Utrecht; Lionel and Alfred de Rothschild, London; Countess of Carnarvon, Newbury, England. *Mellon Collection,* 1937.

AELBERT CUYP · Dutch 1620-1691

Horsemen and Herdsmen with Cattle

Cuyp, soleil déclinant dissous dans l'air limpide
Qu'un vol de ramiers gris trouble comme de l'eau,
Moiteur d'or, nimbe au front d'un bœuf ou d'un bouleau,
Encens bleu des beaux jours fumant sur le coteau,
Ou marais de clarté stagnant dans le ciel vide.
Des cavaliers sont prêts, plume rose au chapeau,
Paume au côté; l'air vif qui fait rose leur peau,
Enfle légèrement leurs fines boucles blondes,
Et, tentés par les champs ardents, les fraîches ondes,
Sans troubler par leur trot les bœufs dont le troupeau
Rêve dans un brouillard d'or pâle et de repos,
Ils partent respirer ces minutes profondes.

[Cuyp! Setting sun melting in the limpid air, like the surface of a pond stirred by a flight of gray doves; liquid gold nimbus on the head of a birch tree or an ox; blue incense of lovely days drifting like smoke over the hillside; tranquil pools of light in the empty sky. Horsemen with their rose-feathered hats are ready, hand on hip. The brisk air which gently colors their skin stirs their silken blond locks. And enticed by glowing fields and cool waters, leaving undisturbed by their hoof-beats the dreamy herd of cattle in the quiet golden haze, they are off to savor these unfathomable moments.]

MARCEL PROUST
Les Plaisirs et les jours (1896)

Canvas. Height 47⅜ in.; width 66½ in. (1.21 x 1.69). Signed. Painted c. 1660-65. The landscape suggests the scenery in the vicinity of Arnheim. Collections: The present painting, with a pendant of a similar subject, is first recorded in the J. van der Linden van Slingeland Collection, Dordrecht, in 1752. In 1785 it was purchased by M. Dubois of Paris. It passed into the Collection of William Smith, who sold it to Edward Gray. In 1834 it was in the Collection of Alexander Baring, who became Lord Ashburton. It remained in the Ashburton Collection until 1907. *Widener Collection,* 1942.

ANTOINE WATTEAU · FRENCH 1684-1721

Italian Comedians

Watteau is the great poet of the eighteenth century. A universe, an entire creation of poetry and dreams, springs from his mind and pervades his work with the elegance of a life of fantasy. A fairyland, a thousand fairylands, have taken wing from the fancy of his brain, the caprice of his art and the freshness of his genius. From the enchanted vision of his imagination, the painter has portrayed an ideal existence, over and apart from his own time, and has created one of those Shakespearean kingdoms, one of those romantic and sparkling countries such as the amorous paradises that visionaries like Polyphilus build on dream clouds for the delicate enjoyment of poetical beings. . . .

It is in his early decorative works, undoubtedly, that Watteau acquired a taste for the theater, in which his able brush was to find so many gay subjects, so many curious scenes, as his brush dramatized the Italian comedians or the French. . . .

Watteau returns to the French comedians once in a while, but less often than to the Italian ones. He paints the motley family of Italian comedians, the true friends and familiars of his brush, in that beautiful, rollicking composition which formed the pendant to that of the French comedians. He paints their picturesque flight from France when driven out by Mme. de Maintenon. He paints their amusements. He paints their nocturnal loves mingled with torchlight serenades. He paints their holidays, their outdoor revels that startle the ducks on a peaceful pond. He paints again and again, on a hundred canvases, their Mezzettino and their Colombina. No matter how shimmering his pictures, we would not be grateful to the chance that led Watteau early in his career to work for an obscure stage-designer, had he been solely concerned with silken costumes and had he not been inspired to make these Transalpine types the poetic actors in his amorous, rustic scenes. In fact, the compositions of this painter no longer seem to belong to the real world, as a result of the introduction of these aerial clowns, these graceful mimes, these music-makers, these elegant incarnations of delicate laughter and refined comedy, these almost immaterial men and women, their reality obscured by myths and symbols. The greensward of his gay love scenes seems to be thronged with allegorical beings, in whom Watteau's wit and light touch have left nothing of the actor who served as model. One has the illusion of a verdant country, peopled by creations of caprice and fantasy.

EDMOND AND JULES DE GONCOURT
L'Art du dix-huitième siècle (1880)

Canvas. Height 25⅛ in.; width 30⅛ in. (0.64 x 0.76). Painted in 1720, this is one of Watteau's last great undertakings. Traveling to England in 1720 in the vain hope of improving his fortune and recovering his health, Watteau painted the present canvas for Dr. Richard Mead, his physician in London. The Italian comedians, a troupe of actors who were disbanded in 1697, when Mme. de Maintenon took offense at their play, *La Fausse Prude,* were once more permitted to give performances in 1716. All the actors in the present canvas have been identified, and were painted by Watteau from drawings or from memory. The same troupe appears in the canvas entitled Gilles in the Louvre. Although the present painting always remained in England, it was widely known through the engravings by Bernard Baron and Pierre-François Bason. A number of drawings, studies for various details of this painting, are cited by Parker. Two of these deal with large groups of figures; one is in the Musée Jacquemart-André and the other is in the Laughlin Collection, Washington. Collections: Dr. Richard Mead, Roger Harene, Sir Thomas Baring, Lord Northbrook, Lord Iveagh, Walter Guinness, London; Baron Thyssen-Bornemisza, Castle Rohoncz, Hungary. *Kress Collection,* 1939.

FRANÇOIS-HUBERT DROUAIS · French 1727-1775

Group Portrait

Society at this time is still imbued with classicism, and is to remain so until after the turn of the century. But it is becoming bored. Its artificial life, with only the pleasures of the mind and of the senses, in which sentiment has no part, begins to seem empty. People begin to be moved by nature, to become enthusiastic about pastoral pleasures and primitive simplicity. Rousseau's eloquence, and the excavation of Herculaneum and Pompeii, will serve only to direct these aspirations toward specific objects. We are just on the eve of the *Nouvelle Héloïse,* and already nature has become fashionable. Thus, Drouais paints the Prince and Princess de Condé in the guise of gardeners; the Prince de Guéménée and Mlle. de Soubise are dressed as vintagers, the de Bouillon children as highlanders making a marmot dance. Thus, François-Hubert seems a very frank spirit, interested in innovation, in touch with the spirit of the times. His accessories show originality. In short, he knows how to adapt the old classic portrait to the taste of the day. With these qualities, supported by great skill in execution, he cannot fail, sooner or later, to become the fashionable painter; he becomes so, very quickly, as a matter of fact. From the year 1757 onward his portraits find great favor with the public. . . .

As one of our present-day portrait painters recently put it, a woman prefers an idealized expression of her physical beauties rather than of her spiritual qualities. That is perhaps why Drouais was the favorite painter of his lovely contemporaries. He knew how to idealize them, he knew how to give their portraits an elegance and distinction that the model no doubt sometimes lacked; in short, he knew how to portray what is known as a great lady, which is something. In this connection one should not fail to cite his portraits of Mme. and Mlle. de Sourches, of Mme. de Pompadour, of Marie Antoinette, of Mme. de Buffon and even those of Mme. du Barry.

He would deserve not to be forgotten, if only for this quality. But he had others as well. His subjects do not pose only for the beholder. They are almost always engaged in doing something, and their activities recall the tastes of the day. . . . His children's portraits, especially, are usually genre pictures. The portrait, thus rendered more intimate, seemed a novelty. And to this must be added the fact that it was always cleverly and effortlessly painted.

C. GABILLOT
Les Trois Drouais
Gazette des Beaux-Arts (1905-1906)

Canvas. Height 96 in.; width 76¾ in. (2.44 x 1.95). Signed, and dated April 1, 1756. The sitters have not been identified. The portrait possibly may represent the family of the Countess de Meulan, as a smaller version by Drouais, labeled La Comtesse de Meulan, is in the possession of that family. The picture is especially interesting as showing an intimate interior of the eighteenth century. Collections: Aristide Bruant, Paris; Lady Swinton of Masham, Yorkshire, England. *Kress Collection,* 1939.

FRANÇOIS BOUCHER · FRENCH 1703-1770
Venus Consoling Love

'Did you regret Mme. de Pompadour? Voltaire wrote to d'Alembert on hearing of her death. Yes, no doubt; for, at the bottom of her heart, *she was one of us;* she protected Letters to the best of her power: behold the end of a beautiful dream!' . . . .

In the entresol over the Marquise's apartments at Versailles lived Doctor Quesnay, her physician, the patron and founder of the sect of the Economists. He was an eccentric, bluff, honest man, still sincere even at Court, serious *with his ape-like air,* inventing ingenious apologues to cover the truth. Whilst the King was in the Marquise's apartments, whilst the Bernis, the Choiseuls, the ministers and courtiers were governing with her, the Encyclopedists and Economists were talking freely on all sorts of things in Quesnay's entresol, and disposing of the future. The Marquise seems to have felt that storm-clouds were gathering over her head, when she said: *Après moi le déluge!* . . . .

The privacy of letters was then very little observed, and the Superintendent of the Post-Office came regularly every week and brought to the King and Mme. de Pompadour the extracts which had been made from them. When Doctor Quesnay saw him pass, he would fall into such a fury of passion at that *infamous* ministry, as he called it, that he *foamed at the mouth:* 'I would as soon dine with the hangman, he would say, as with the Superintendent of the Post-Office.' These conversations took place in the apartments of the King's mistress, and without any danger, and that went on for twenty years. M. de Marigni, Mme. de Pompadour's brother, a man of merit and worthy of his sister in more than one respect, was contented with saying: 'It is honesty that is finding a vent, and not ill-will.'

One day when this same M. de Marigni was in Quesnay's apartments, the conversation turned to M. de Choiseul:

'He is no better than a dandy, said the Doctor, and if he were prettier, he might have been one of Henri III's minions.' The Marquis de Mirabeau entered (the father of the great tribune) and M. de La Rivière. 'This kingdom is in a very bad way, said Mirabeau; there are neither vigorous opinions nor money to make them good.' 'It can only be regenerated by a conquest as in China, or by some great inner upheaval; but woe to those who are there! the French people can strike hard.' These words made me tremble, adds the good Mme. du Hausset, who hands down the story, and I hastened to leave the room. M. de Marigni did the same, without appearing to be affected by what was said.'

Bring these prophetic words together with those which escaped Louis XV himself on the subject of the resistance of Parliament: 'Things will go on as they are as long as I live.' That was the end of his world.

C. A. SAINTE-BEUVE
Causeries du lundi (1850)

Canvas. Height 43 in.; width 33½ in. (1.09 x 0.86). Signed, and dated 1751. This painting and a pendant, The Toilet of Venus in the Metropolitan Museum, New York, are in all probability the two pictures listed as Item 78 in the inventory (1764) of Mme. de Pompadour. They next appear in 1782, in the sale of the collection of Mme. de Pompadour's brother, Marquis de Ménars (Marigny). The present painting later passed to the following collections: H. Cousin, Paris; Baron Alfred de Rothschild, Buckinghamshire, England; and the Marchioness Curzon of Kedleston. *Gift of Chester Dale,* 1943.

FRANÇOIS BOUCHER · FRENCH 1703-1770

Madame Bergeret

Boucher is one of those men who symbolize, express, personify, or embody the taste of an epoch. In him, French taste of the eighteenth century is disclosed in all the distinctiveness of its character. Boucher will remain not only the painter, but also the eye-witness, the representative, and the embodiment of his age.

Neither the *grand siècle* nor Louis XIV had favored reality in art. The patronage of Versailles and the plaudits of the public stimulated the efforts of literature, painting, sculpture, architecture and the energies of genius and talent towards a false grandeur and a conventional nobility, which confined Beauty in solemnity and rules of ceremony. A kind of sublimity of ostentation, pomp and dignity had dazzled the spirit of France; shutting its ears to the language of Shakespeare and its eyes to the pictures of Teniers, French society believed that in fictitious splendor it had found a supreme aesthetic canon, an absolute ideal.

When the age of Louis XIV was succeeded by that of Louis XV, when frivolous France emerged from pompous France, and around a more human monarchy things and people became smaller, the ideal of art remained artificial and conventional. The majestic yielded to the pleasurable. Everywhere there spread a refined elegance and a delicate sensuousness, which the age described as "the quintessence of the exquisite," "the brilliance of charm and grace," and "the embellishment of merriment and love-making." The theater, the book, the picture, the statue, the house, the suite — everything shared the adornment, the coquetry and gracefulness of a delightful decadence. In these breezy hours of her history, grace became the symbol and allurement of France, the essence of her thought and inspiration, the tone of her manners, the school of her fashions. Grace is the spirit of the times, and the genius of Boucher.

EDMOND AND JULES DE GONCOURT
L'Art du dix-huitième siècle (1880)

Canvas. Height 56½ in.; width 41½ in. (1.44 x 1.06). Signed, and dated 1746. This portrait of Mme. Bergeret is probably the earliest of the relatively small group of portraits known to have been painted by Boucher. It hung in the boudoir of Mme. Bergeret, according to an inventory made in 1785. Two of the foremost patrons of Boucher and of his pupil Fragonard were her husband, Jacques Onésime Bergeret, and her brother, Jean-Claude, Abbé de Saint-Non. The Bergerets seem to have been among the first to recognize Boucher's talent, and it is quite probable that through them the young artist was brought to the attention of Mme. de Pompadour, for whom, a few years later, he was to do some of his most representative work. Collections: Jacques Onésime Bergeret, Ange Philibert de la Girennerie, Poisson de la Chabeaussière, Cotillon de Torcy, Le Bos de Sainte Croix, Fontaine de Resbecq. *Kress Collection*, 1939.

JEAN-BAPTISTE GREUZE · French 1725-1805

Monsieur de La Live de Jully

This artist, who is not lacking in self-esteem, in which he is indeed justified, proposed to paint an historical picture and to earn the right to all the honors of his profession. He chose for his subject: Septimius Severus Reproaching His Son Caracalla for Having Made an Attempt on His Life in the Scottish Mountain Passes. . . .

The day came when this picture, executed with the greatest care, and heralded by the artist himself as a work to rival the best that Poussin had done, having been inspected by the director and some of the commissioners, was presented at the Academy. You can imagine that it was not examined with sympathetic eyes, since Greuze had long shown such frank and decided contempt for his colleagues and their works.

This is the procedure in such matters. The Academy convenes, the picture is displayed on an easel in the middle of the room: the academicians examine it. Meanwhile, the candidate, alone, in another room, paces about or sits, awaiting their judgment. Greuze, if I am not much mistaken, was not greatly concerned as to their decision.

After an hour, the double doors opened and Greuze entered. The director said: "Sir, the Academy receives you. Come forward and take the oath." Greuze, delighted, complies with all the formalities of admittance. When they are over, the director says to him: "Sir, the Academy has received you, but as a painter of genre; it has taken into consideration your previous works, which are excellent, and it has closed its eyes to this one, which is worthy neither of it nor of you."

At this moment, Greuze, seeing his hopes blighted, lost his head, acted like a child by upholding the excellence of his picture, and at one point La Grénée pulled his pencil out of his pocket in order to demonstrate to him on the canvas itself the inaccuracies of his figures.

What would anyone else have done? you will ask me. Another, I for instance, would have pulled out a knife and ripped the picture to pieces. Then he would have put the frame about his neck, and, carrying it off with him, would have told the Academy that he wished to be neither a genre painter nor an historical painter. He would have gone home to frame the marvelous heads of Papinian and of the senator, which he would have taken pains to spare amidst the destruction of the rest, and would have left the Academy confounded and dishonored. Yes, my friend, dishonored; since Greuze's picture, before it was presented, was considered a masterpiece and the scraps of it preserved would have perpetuated this presumption forever; those superb scraps would have suggested the beauty of the rest, and the greatest collector would have acquired them for their weight in gold. . . .

That is the summary of the Greuze incident, which has caused a great stir here.

DENIS DIDEROT
Salon de 1769

Canvas. Height 45⅞ in.; width 34⅞ in. (1.17 x 0.89). Exhibited at the Salon of 1759, this portrait, one of Greuze's finest achievements, exemplifies Diderot's reference to the "marvelous heads" that would have been worth "their weight in gold," and proves, as Diderot implies, that Greuze's real ability lay in portraiture. The sitter, a close friend of Mme. de Pompadour, was one of the earliest patrons of Greuze, as well as a notable collector of eighteenth-century art, and the author of a history of French painting. Collections: La Live de Jully, Laborde, Fitz-James, Feltre, Goyon, Montesquieu-Fezensac, Paris. *Kress Collection*, 1939.

JEAN-BAPTISTE SIMEON CHARDIN · French 1699-1779

The Young Governess

They trudged past acres of canvas, through one room after another, for Lydia had some difficulty in finding her way; but finally she stopped him in front of a small picture that you might easily have missed if you had not been looking for it.

"Chardin," he said. "Yes, I've seen that before."

"But have you ever looked at it?". . . .

Lydia's voice was tremulous and now the tears flowed from her eyes. She brushed them away impatiently.

"And isn't it wonderful that with those simple objects, with his painter's exquisite sensibility, moved by the charity in his heart, that funny, dear old man should have made something so beautiful that it breaks you? It was as though, unconsciously perhaps, hardly knowing what he was doing, he wanted to show you that if you only have enough love, if you only have enough sympathy, out of pain and distress and unkindness, out of all the evil of the world, you can create beauty."

She was silent and for long stood looking at the little picture. Charley looked at it too, but with perplexity. It was a very good picture; he hadn't really given it more than a glance before, and he was glad Lydia had drawn his attention to it; in some odd way it was rather moving; but of course he could never have seen in it all she saw. Strange, unstable woman! It was rather embarrassing that she should cry in a public gallery; they did put you in an awkward position, these Russians; but who would have thought a picture could affect anyone like that? He remembered his mother's story of how a student friend of his grandfather's had fainted when he first saw the Odalisque of Ingres; but that was away back in the nineteenth century, they were very romantic and emotional in those days. Lydia turned to him with a sunny smile on her lips. It disconcerted him to see with what suddenness she could go from tears to laughter.

"Shall we go now?" she said.

"But don't you want to see any more pictures?"

"Why? I've seen one. I feel happy and peaceful. What could I get if I saw another?"

"Oh, all right."

It seemed a very odd way of doing a picture gallery. After all, they hadn't looked at the Watteaus or the Fragonards. His mother was bound to ask him if he'd seen the Embarkation for Cythera.

W. Somerset Maugham
Christmas Holiday (1939)

Canvas. Height 23 in.; width 29¼ in. (0.58 x 0.74). Signed at lower center. Painted c. 1739. One of several versions of the theme, of which two are in the National Galleries of England and Ireland. One of these pictures was exhibited in the Salon du Louvre of 1740, and engraved the same year in reverse by Lépicié. Although the quotation above refers to another painting, the qualities indicated by Maugham appear in all the great works by Chardin. Collections: Vicomte du Curel, Paris. *Mellon Collection,* 1937.

JEAN-HONORE FRAGONARD · French 1732-1806

The Visit to the Nursery

Leaf through all the drawings of Fragonard; scattered sheets, fleeting thoughts in which his work is enshrined. . . . The theme of childhood recurs everywhere; childhood smiles from every page. It accounts for the freshness, the youth, the innocence of all these little pictures. The child, the little one in his brief bodice, romping and dancing in the sun with something of the airiness and nudity of a young god; the child with his tiny hands wandering caressingly over his mother's face and breast; the child with his heart-shaped mouth; the child with his dog and donkey, riding on their backs or clinging to their necks; the child all white in his huge little nightshirt; on top of a pyramid of children eyeing a pan of fritters; the fair-haired, curly-headed child, doll in arms, preaching from a sideboard with the air of a small waxen Saint John — all these little ones bring the glow and bustle of Paradise into Fragonard's scenes. When they are very little, Fragonard shows them slumbering in the midst of a flowering garden, under a mother's tender caresses, in a cradle that seems to have blossomed amid the clusters of roses that shed their petals over it. When the children are a little older, the painter shows them standing upon the tub of an orange tree, wrapped by maternal hands in folds from which only their little faces emerge. Sometimes the painter has them climb into their mother's lap like ascending angels. It seems as if he takes a fatherly joy in grouping these little ones, in mustering them in ranks, in making them play and turn somersaults. One might say that he jounced his compositions on his knees. How well he catches the ages of all these gay, lively, rosy and jolly creatures, these very little boys, these pretty, little bits of girls, these budding women! These are not the children that Chardin paints, already serious, growing up in the somber gloom of tiny-paned rooms, in the sober tutelage of a restricted and severe life. They are really Fragonard's family, the children of his genius — these friendly little demons, beaming, radiant, showing cupid's knees between their little trousers and their rolled stockings, spoiled children of happiness and countryside, of love and of nature, blest offspring of shepherdesses and great lords, born, one might imagine, of the lively scenes of our painter, of the pairs of lovers whom his brush tumbles on bales of hay.

EDMOND AND JULES DE GONCOURT
L'Art du dix-huitième siècle (1880)

Canvas. Height 28⅞ in.; width 36¼ in. (0.73 x 0.92). Painted before 1784. Fragonard did many family scenes, which his own domestic happiness enabled him to treat with unusual sympathy, and which, under the influence of contemporary literature, reflected the revived emphasis on family life that appeared during the second half of the eighteenth century. Tradition has it that The Visit to the Nursery was derived from Saint-Lambert's romance *Sara Th...* (1766). A preliminary drawing and a sketch were made for the painting, which was engraved by Charles Courtry. Collections: Le Roy de Senneville, Paris; Jules Burat, Versailles; Mme. Burat, Paris. *Kress Collection*, 1939.

JEAN-HONORE FRAGONARD · FRENCH 1732-1806

A Game of Hot Cockles

Whereas the plastic art of the Gothic age is architectonic ornament — rows of human figures — through and through, the plastic art of the Rococo period is a significant example of an art which is only plastic superficially, while in reality it is under the domination of Music — which is its opposite in the circle of the arts — and is speaking in the language of musical form. This reveals the degree to which it is possible for the technique that governs the foreground of artistic life to be in contradiction with the spirit of the world of forms which this technique creates (*pace* the usual aesthetic theory which assumes that spirit and technique stand to each other in the relation of a cause and an effect). Compare the crouching Venus of Coyzevox (A.D. 1686) in the Louvre with her Hellenic forerunner in the Vatican, and you will see the difference between plastic art treated as music and plastic art working in its own right. In Coyzevox's work, the sense of movement, the flow of the lines, and the fluidity that has been imparted to the very essence of the stone — which, like porcelain, has somehow lost its solidity and mass — can be described most aptly in musical terms: staccato, accelerando, andante, allegro. Hence the feeling that somehow the close-grained marble is here out of place. Hence, too, the altogether un-Hellenic reliance on effects of light and shade: a device which corresponds to what has been the leading principle of oil-painting since Titian. The quality which the Eighteenth Century called colour — whether in an engraving or in a drawing or in a group of statuary — really means music. This quality governs the painting of Watteau and Fragonard and the art of the Gobelins and Pastelle. Do we not talk, from that day to this, of "colour-tones" and "tone-colours"? And is this not a recognition of an equivalence finally attained between two arts that are superficially so different? And are not all such designations meaningless in reference to all Hellenic Art? Music even succeeded in recasting, in its own spirit, the Baroque architecture of Bernini. It re-cast it into Rococo; and the transcendental Rococo ornamentation is "played" over by lights which are virtually musical tones, and which perform the function of resolving roofs, walls, arches and everything that is constructive and concrete into polyphony and harmony: an architectural music whose trills, cadences and passaggios carry to the point of identity the assimilation of the architectural semantic of these halls and galleries to the music which was conceived for them. Dresden and Vienna are the homes of this late and shortlived wonderland of chamber music and billowy furniture and mirror-rooms and pastoral poetry and porcelain-groups. This is the last expression of the Western soul: an expression of autumnal ripeness with a touch of autumn sunshine. The Vienna of the Vienna Congress saw it die and disappear.

OSWALD SPENGLER
Der Untergang des Abendlandes (1920)

Canvas. Height 45½ in.; width 36¼ in. (1.15 x 0.92). Painted between 1767 and 1773, as a pendant to A Game of Horse and Rider, also in the Kress Collection, National Gallery of Art. These paintings, and The Swing in the Wallace Collection, London, were executed for Baron de Saint-Julien. The marble statue of the Cupid on the right of the picture, which also appears in The Swing, is Falconet's famous L'Amour Menaçant, executed for Mme. de Pompadour and exhibited in the Salon du Louvre of 1757. The picture reproduced on the right — one of the great masterpieces of eighteenth-century painting — exemplifies the essence of the rococo style, as described by Spengler. Falconet's statue illustrates, even better than the Coysevox Venus mentioned by Spengler, the change from the classical to the rococo. Collections: Baron de Saint-Julien, Jenny Coulon, E. Pereire, Comte Pillet-Will, Paris. *Kress Collection*, 1939.

GIOVANNI BATTISTA TIEPOLO · Venetian 1696-1770

Timocleia and the Thracian Commander

He is a great painter and exclusively a painter. He is intoxicated with painting. His ecstasies demand church and palace ceilings, throne rooms, ceremonial stairways, vast expanses, where his genius suddenly bursts forth like great clashes of golden cymbals. . . .

Dishevelled, distracted, he rushes about like a whirlwind through space. Arms and legs in the air, impossible foreshortenings, draperies and hair flying in the wind, furiously galloping horses and plunging chariots, buildings turned upside down, clusters of tumbling bodies, great clouds rent asunder and light flooding down in torrents — such are his ceilings. They are like the exploits of heroes. . . .

And what magnificent gaiety! It is a resounding outburst, the essence of youth and merriment in an explosion of beauty. Above all, it is light — all the light of the skies, all the light of the seas, all the light of Venice — which has flooded his eyes, and permeated the very marrow of his bones. . . . He does not paint ideas, scarcely even forms — but light. His ceilings glow like the bird-filled sky, and his poems seem written in clouds. *Fiat lux!* Let there be light! Light is fairer than all things, more beautiful than man or woman. It is the fairest of all God's creatures and Tiepolo knows all its tricks and triumphs.

He knows the resplendence of the out-of-doors. He is drunk with the transparency of the atmosphere. He sports in the magic of the enveloping air and plays with reflections like a tight-rope walker with his golden balls. The golden grays, the pearly whites, the warm blond tones, are all familiar to him. He knows the glint of a bit of straw in a stable, the daylight that seems to fall from lamps of opal, and the rosy rays that steal from quivering dawns. Amber brightness, blushing pallor, flashes of rosy pink and pearl, everything in the world that is fluid and diaphanous, all the iridescent secrets of the waves, of the air, and of the clouds, everything that glistens and shimmers — all this he knows.

He is not merely a great eighteenth-century painter; he is simply a great painter. He is the aristocratic artist, working for patricians who perform great deeds and commission frescoes. He is the contemporary of everything in Venice that still measures up to the memory of the great past. His place is beside the Doge Foscarini, the Admiral Emo, the musician Marcello. He is the citizen of the opulent sovereign state, at whose feet Neptune poured forth his conch of coins, of pearls, and of corals — a scene Tiepolo has recalled over a door in the Scrutinio. In his work, tradition survives; the Renaissance continues; the Decadence is clothed in majesty. An age which produced such a master remains great.

Philippe Monnier
Venise au XVIIIe siècle (1907)

Canvas. Height 55¼ in.; width 43⅛ in. (1.40 x 1.10). Painted c. 1755, and originally part of the decoration of a room in the Palazzo Barbaro, Venice. The central section, now in the Metropolitan Museum, New York, represents the Glorification of Francesco Barbaro. Arranged around it were the present painting and three others, traditionally entitled: Tarquinius and Lucretia, Vestals Sacrificing, and the Rejected Proposal. Collections: Palazzo Barbaro, Venice; Duc de Camondo, Baron Adolphe de Rothschild, Paris; Baron von Springer, Dr. Kranz, Stephan von Auspitz, Vienna. *Kress Collection*, 1939.

GOYA · Spanish 1746-1828

The Marquesa de Pontejos

Francisco Goya y Lucientes can rightly be called the last Spanish painter; he brings to an end that vigorous generation of artists of the sixteenth and seventeenth centuries; he is still recognizable as a descendant of Velázquez. After him come the Aparicios and the Lopez. The decadence of art is complete: the cycle is closed! Who will ever reopen it?

Goya is, indeed, a strange painter — a most singular genius! Never was originality more decided — never was a Spanish painter more local. One of Goya's sketches, four touches of his etcher's needle in a cloud of aquatint, tells you more about the manners of the country than the most lengthy description. By his adventurous mode of living, his impetuosity, and his manifold talents, Goya seems to belong to the greatest ages of art; and yet he is, in a sense, a contemporary, having died at Bordeaux in 1828. . . .

His taste for drawing and painting developed at an early age. He traveled, studied for some time at Rome, and returned to Spain, where he soon made a fortune at the court of Charles IV, who conferred on him the title of Painter to the King. He was received by the Queen, the Prince of Benavente and the Duchess of Alba, and led the lordly life of a Rubens, a Van Dyck or a Velázquez — that mode of existence so highly favorable to the development of a pictorial genius. . . .

Goya was very prolific; he produced sacred subjects, frescoes, portraits, and genre pictures, etchings, aquatints, and lithographs. In everything he did, even in the slightest sketches, he gave proof of a most vigorous talent; the lion's claw marks his most casual works. His talent, although singularly original, is a strange mixture of Velázquez, Rembrandt, and Reynolds; recalling in turn, or even at the same time, all of these masters, but as the son reminds you of his forebears, without any servile imitation. . . .

Goya is a composite of Rembrandt, Watteau and the ribald dreams of Rabelais; a strange mixture! Add to all this a strong Spanish flavor, a stiff dose of the *picaresque* spirit of Cervantes, as in the portraits of the Escalanta and the Gananciosa, in *Rinconete y Cortadillo,* and even then you will have but an imperfect notion of Goya's talent. . . .

The ancient art of Spain is buried in Goya's tomb. Now lost forever is all that world of toreros, majos and mañolas, of smugglers, robbers, alguazils and sorceresses; in a word, all the local color of the Peninsula. He came just in time to gather up and perpetuate all of this. He thought that he was merely producing so many capricious sketches. He was, in fact, drawing the portrait and writing the history of the Spain of olden days, in the belief that he was serving the ideas and beliefs of modern times.

THÉOPHILE GAUTIER
Fran^co Goya y Lucientes
Le Cabinet de l'amateur et de l'antiquaire (1842)

Canvas. Height 83 in.; width 49½ in. (2.11 x 1.26). Painted 1785-1790. The design of the portrait suggests the probable influence on Goya's early work of engravings after Gainsborough and Reynolds. Collections: Marqués de Miraflores y de Pontejos, Madrid. *Mellon Collection,* 1937.

128

THOMAS GAINSBOROUGH · British 1727-1788

Mrs. Richard Brinsley Sheridan

It must be remembered that the style and department of art which Gainsborough chose, and in which he so much excelled, did not require that he should go out of his own country for the objects of his study; they were every where about him; he found them in the streets, and in the fields; and from the models thus accidentally found, he selected with great judgment such as suited his purpose. As his studies were directed to the living world principally, he did not pay a general attention to the works of the various masters, though they are, in my opinion, always of great use, even when the character of our subject requires us to depart from some of their principles. It cannot be denied, that excellence in the department of the art which he professed may exist without them; that in such subjects, and in the manner that belongs to them, the want of them is supplied, and more than supplied, by natural sagacity, and a minute observation of particular nature. If Gainsborough did not look at nature with a poet's eye, it must be acknowledged that he saw her with the eye of a painter; and gave a faithful, if not a poetical, representation of what he had before him.

Though he did not much attend to the works of the great historical painters of former ages, yet he was well aware that the language of the art, — the art of imitation, — must be learned somewhere; and as he knew that he could not learn it in an equal degree from his contemporaries, he very judiciously applied himself to the Flemish School, who are undoubtedly the greatest masters of one necessary branch of art; and he did not need to go out of his own country for examples of that school: from that he learnt the harmony of colouring, the management and disposition of light and shadow, and every means which the masters of it practised, to ornament and give splendour to their works. And to satisfy himself as well as others, how well he knew the mechanism and artifice which they employed to bring out that tone of colour which we so much admired in their works, he occasionally made copies from Rubens, Teniers, and Vandyck, which it would be no disgrace to the most accurate connoisseur to mistake, at the first sight, for the works of those masters. What he thus learned, he applied to the originals of nature, which he saw with his own eyes; and imitated, not in the manner of those masters, but in his own.

Whether he most excelled in portraits, landscapes, or fancy-pictures, it is difficult to determine: whether his portraits were most admirable for exact truth of resemblance, or his landscapes for a portrait-like representation of nature, such as we see in the works of Rubens, Ruysdaal, and others of those schools. In his fancy-pictures, when he had fixed on his object of imitation, whether it was the mean and vulgar form of a wood-cutter, or a child of an interesting character, as he did not attempt to raise the one, so neither did he lose any of the natural grace and elegance of the other; such a grace, and such an elegance, as are more frequently found in cottages than in courts. This excellence was his own, the result of his particular observation and taste.

Sir Joshua Reynolds
The Discourses (1798)

Canvas. Height 86½ in.; width 60½ in. (2.20 x 1.54). One of several portraits of Mrs. Sheridan by Gainsborough. This appears to be the canvas which is recorded as having been in the artist's studio during the years 1785 and 1786. At the autumn exhibition of 1786 in the Gainsborough Gallery, Bate (Whitley, *Thomas Gainsborough*) stated that the painting still lacked the lambs in the background which the artist was about to add to give the picture "an air more pastoral than it at present possesses." Engraved by Gainsborough Dupont before 1797. Collections: Baron Nathaniel Rothschild, London. *Mellon Collection*, 1937.

SIR JOSHUA REYNOLDS · British 1723-1792

Lady Caroline Howard

Even in portraits, the grace, and, we may add, the likeness, consists more in taking the general air, than in observing the exact similitude of every feature.

Thus figures must have a ground whereon to stand; they must be cloathed; there must be a back-ground; there must be light and shadow: but none of these ought to appear to have taken up any part of the artist's attention. They should be so managed as not even to catch that of the spectator. We know well enough, when we analyze a piece, the difficulty and the subtilty with which an artist adjusts the back-ground, drapery, and masses of light; we know that a considerable part of the grace and effect of his picture depends upon them; but this art is so much concealed, even to a judicious eye, that no remains of any of these subordinate parts occur to the memory when the picture is not present.

The great end of the art is to strike the imagination. The Painter therefore is to make no ostentation of the means by which this is done; the spectator is only to feel the result in his bosom. An inferior artist is unwilling that any part of his industry should be lost upon the spectator. He takes as much pains to discover, as the greater artist does to conceal, the marks of his subordinate assiduity. In works of the lower kind, every thing appears studied, and encumbered; it is all boastful art, and open affectation. The ignorant often part from such pictures with wonder in their mouths, and indifference in their hearts. . . .

A painter must compensate the natural deficiencies of his art. He has but one sentence to utter, but one moment to exhibit. He cannot, like the poet or historian, expatiate, and impress the mind with great veneration for the character of the hero or saint he represents, though he lets us know at the same time, that the saint was deformed, or the hero lame. The Painter has no other means of giving an idea of the dignity of the mind, but by that external appearance which grandeur of thought does generally, though not always, impress on the countenance; and by that correspondence of figure to sentiment and situation, which all men wish, but cannot command. The Painter, who may in this one particular attain with ease what others desire in vain, ought to give all that he possibly can, since there are so many circumstances of true greatness that he cannot give at all. He cannot make his hero talk like a great man; he must make him look like one. For which reason, he ought to be well studied in the analysis of those circumstances, which constitute dignity of appearance in real life.

SIR JOSHUA REYNOLDS
The Discourses (1798)

Canvas. Height 56¼ in.; width 44½ in. (1.43 x 1.13). Painted c. 1778. Engraved in that year by Valentine Green. First exhibited in the Royal Academy in 1779. A similar pose and setting were used by the artist in other paintings of children, notably in the Age of Innocence, of the National Gallery, London. The present portrait has retained its clear, fresh color to a degree rare in Reynolds' work. Collections: Earl of Carlisle, Castle Howard, England. *Mellon Collection, 1937.*

Lady Caroline Howard
Lady Cawdor.

GEORGE ROMNEY · BRITISH 1734-1802

Mrs. Davenport

The emoluments of portrait painting may be said both to support and to ruin a great artist: They afford him affluence, but they impede his progress in that higher field of imagination, which promises a richer harvest of delight and honor. Romney felt and lamented the fetters of his profession, and often pleased himself with a prospect of shaking them off, but he was not aware of the infinite efforts required to break the golden fetters of custom. He was not dazzled, or enslaved by the gold he gained, for he had a spirit superior to such bribery, and he often threw money away as rapidly as he acquired it; but he really had a pleasure in painting a new face, exclusive of all pecuniary considerations, and his heart was so tenderly sympathetic, that if he had resolved most solemnly never to paint another portrait for any fresh sitter, yet a lover, begging a likeness of his favorite nymph, or a mother, requesting a resemblance of a darling child, might have melted, in a few moments, his sternest resolution. If the facility, with which he sympathized in the feelings of those, who required his attention, often led him to find in portrait-painting much cordial gratification, unmixed with ideas of interest; on the other hand it tormented him exceedingly, when he was desired to preserve an exact likeness, and yet to bestow considerable character on a countenance, to which nature had given very little or none. On such occasions he was apt to be very faithful in his representation of life, and once when the portrait of a simple gentleman was sent back to him to receive a more animated countenance, I remember to have seen the artist in much ludicrous perplexity from having vainly tried to make a simpleton, most truly delineated, retain his own features, and yet look like a man of sense. I could not on this occasion apply to him an admirable compliment addrest by Dryden to his friend Kneller;

> *"Thus thou sometimes art forc'd to draw a fool,*
> *But so his follies in thy posture sink,*
> *The senseless idiot seems at last to think."*

For in the portrait alluded to, a weakness of understanding was still visible, after repeated endeavours of the mortified painter to give his too faithful inanimate image the requested air of intelligence.

WILLIAM HAYLEY
The Life of George Romney (1809)

Canvas. Height 30 in.; width 25 in. (0.76 x 0.64). The sittings for this portrait are recorded in Romney's diaries during the years 1782-1784. Engraved by John Jones in 1784. Collections: Davies Davenport; Sir William Bromley Davenport, Capesthorne Hall, Cheshire. *Mellon Collection*, 1937.

SIR HENRY RAEBURN · British 1756-1823

Miss Eleanor Urquhart

He looked people shrewdly between the eyes, surprised their manners in their face, and had possessed himself of what was essential in their character before they had been many minutes in his studio. What he was so swift to perceive, he conveyed to the canvas almost in the moment of conception. He had never any difficulty, he said, about either hands or faces. About draperies or light or composition, he might see room for hesitation or after-thought. But a face or a hand was something plain and legible. There were no two ways about it, any more than about the person's name. And so each of his portraits are not only (in Doctor Johnson's phrase . . . .) "a piece of history," but a piece of biography into the bargain. It is devoutly to be wished that all biography were equally amusing, and carried its own credentials equally upon its face. These portraits are racier than many anecdotes, and more complete than many a volume of sententious memoirs. You can see whether you get a stronger and clearer idea of Robertson the historian from Raeburn's palette or Dugald Stewart's woolly and evasive periods. And then the portraits are both signed and counter-signed. For you have, first, the authority of the artist, whom you recognize as no mean critic of the looks and manners of men; and next you have the tacit acquiescence of the subject, who sits looking out upon you with inimitable innocence, and apparently under the impression that he is in a room by himself. For Raeburn could plunge at once through all the constraint and embarrassment of the sitter, and present the face, clear, open, and intelligent as at the most disengaged moments.

Robert Louis Stevenson
Virginibus Puerisque (1881)

Canvas. Height 29½ in.; width 24½ in. (0.75 x 0.62). Painted c. 1795. The present portrait is characteristic of Raeburn's first manner. The paint is applied so thinly as to be transparent, and broad surfaces of light are contrasted with sharply outlined shadows. In style and in general treatment the portrait is closely related to those in the National Gallery, London, of Miss Forbes and Mrs. Lauzun, the latter painted in 1795. Collections: Captain Michael Pollard-Urquhart, Craigston, Scotland. *Mellon Collection,* 1937.

BENJAMIN WEST · AMERICAN 1738-1820

Colonel Guy Johnson

Mr. West (who, as I have already mentioned, had married one of my relations) had bought his house, I believe, not long after he came to England; and he had added a gallery at the back of it, terminating in a couple of lofty rooms. . . . The two rooms contained the largest of his pictures; and in the farther one, after stepping softly down the gallery, as if reverencing the dumb life on the walls, you generally found the mild and quiet artist at his work; happy, for he thought himself immortal.

I need not enter into the merits of an artist who is so well known, and has been so often criticized. He was a man with regular, mild features; and, though of Quaker origin, had the look of what he was, a painter to a court. . . . Yet this man, so well bred, and so indisputably clever in his art (whatever might be the amount of his genius), had received so careless, or so homely an education when a boy, that he could hardly read. He pronounced also some of his words, in reading, with a puritanical barbarism, such as *haive* for *have,* as some people pronounce when they sing psalms. But this was, perhaps, an American custom. . . . Mr. West would talk of his art all day long, painting all the while. On other subjects he was not so fluent; and on political and religious matters he tried hard to maintain the reserve common with those about a court. He succeeded ill in both. There were always strong suspicions of his leaning to his native side in politics; and during Bonaparte's triumph, he could not contain his enthusiasm for the Republican chief, going even to Paris to pay him his homage, when First Consul. The admiration of high colours and powerful effects, natural to a painter, was too strong for him. How he managed this matter with the higher powers in England I cannot say. Probably he was the less heedful, inasmuch as he was not very carefully paid. I believe he did a great deal for George the Third with little profit. Mr. West certainly kept his love for Bonaparte no secret; and it was no wonder, for the latter expressed admiration of his pictures. The artist thought the conqueror's smile enchanting, and that he had the handsomest leg he had ever seen. He was present when the "Venus de' Medici" was talked of, the French having just taken possession of her. Bonaparte, Mr. West said, turned round to those about him, and said, with his eyes lit up, "She's coming!" as if he had been talking of a living person. I believe he retained for the Emperor the love that he had had for the First Consul, a wedded love, "for better, for worse." However, I believe also that he retained it after the Emperor's downfall — which is not what every painter did.

LEIGH HUNT
Autobiography (1860)

Canvas. Height 79¾ in.; width 54½ in. (2.03 x 1.38). Painted c. 1775. Colonel Johnson was one of the first superintendents of Indian affairs. Beside him stands his devoted friend, Captain Joseph Brant, who was known in his own language as Thayendanegea. Collections: Dina E. Brown, Henfield, England. *Mellon Collection, 1940.*

JOHN SINGLETON COPLEY · AMERICAN 1738-1815
The Copley Family

Those who desire to know the modes of study, the peculiar habits, the feelings and opinions, likings and dislikings, of Copley, cannot, I fear, be gratified. No one lives now who could tell us of his early days, when the boy, on the wild shores of America, achieved works of surpassing beauty; he is but remembered in his declining years, when the world had sobered down his mood, and the ecstasy of the blood was departed. He has been represented to me by some as a peevish and peremptory man, while others describe him as mild and unassuming. Man has many moods, and they have all, I doubt not, spoken the truth of their impressions. I can depend more upon the authority which says, he was fond of books, a lover of history, and well acquainted with poetry, especially the divine works of Milton. These he preferred to exercise either on foot or on horseback, when labour at the easel was over — and this bookish turn has been talked of as injurious to his health; but no one has much right to complain of shortness of years, who lives to see out threescore and eighteen.

He sometimes made experiments in colours: the methods of the Greeks, the elder Italians, and the schools of Florence and Venice, he was long in quest of; and he wrote out receipts for composing those lustrous hues in which Titian and Correggio excelled. For the worth of his discoveries, read not his receipts, but look at his works.

ALLAN CUNNINGHAM
The Lives of the Most Eminent British Painters,
Sculptors, and Architects (1832)

Stuart used to tell me, that no man ever knew how to *manage paint* better than Copley. I suppose he meant that *firm,* artist-like manner in which it was applied to the canvas; but he said he was very tedious in his practice. He once visited Copley in his painting-room, and being a good deal of a beau!! Copley asked him to stand for him, that he might paint a bit of a ruffle-shirt that stuck out of his bosom. Not thinking that it would take more than a few minutes, he complied. But after standing a long time, and growing uneasy, Copley began to apologize. 'No consequence at all,' said Stuart, 'I beg you would finish — do all you can do to it now, for this is the last time you ever get me into such a scrape.'

HENRY SARGENT (c. 1833)

Canvas. Height 72⅞ in.; width 89⅞ in. (1.85 x 2.28). Painted shortly after Copley's family had arrived in England, where they had fled at the outbreak of the American Revolution. Copley himself appears at the upper left. Below him sits his father-in-law, Richard Clarke, agent of the East India Company, to whom was consigned the cargo of tea thrown into the harbor at the Boston Tea Party. Clarke holds on his lap Copley's youngest son, Jonathan. Next to him stands Elizabeth, and to the right are John Singleton Copley, Jr., afterwards Lord Lyndhurst, Mrs. Copley, and Mary, the younger daughter. Collections: John Singleton Copley, Lord Lyndhurst, London. *Copley Amory Collection.*

GILBERT STUART · AMERICAN 1755-1828

George Washington

Although distrusting my ability to give an adequate account of the personal appearance of Col. George Washington, late Commander of the Virginia Provincial troops, I shall, as you request, attempt the portraiture. He may be described as being as straight as an Indian, measuring six feet two inches in his stockings, and weighing 175 pounds when he took his seat in the House of Burgesses in 1759. His frame is padded with well-developed muscles, indicating great strength. His bones and joints are large, as are his feet and hands. He is wide shouldered, but has not a deep or round chest; is neat waisted, but is broad across the hips, and has rather long legs and arms. His head is well shaped though not large, but is gracefully poised on a superb neck. A large and straight rather than a prominent nose; blue-gray penetrating eyes, which were widely separated and overhung by a heavy brow. His face is long rather than broad, with high round cheek bones, and terminates in a good firm chin. He has a clear though rather colorless pale skin, which burns with the sun. A pleasing, benevolent, though a commanding countenance, dark brown hair, which he wears in a cue. His mouth is large and generally firmly closed, but which from time to time discloses some defective teeth. His features are regular and placid, with all the muscles of his face under perfect control, though flexible and expressive of deep feeling when moved by emotions. In conversation he looks you full in the face, is deliberate, deferential and engaging. His voice is agreeable rather than strong. His demeanor at all times composed and dignified. His movements and gestures are graceful, his walk majestic, and he is a splendid horseman.

CAPTAIN GEORGE MERCER
Letter (1760)

General Washington throws off the Hero and takes up the chatty agreeable Companion — he can be down right impudent sometimes — such impudence, Fanny, as you and I like.

A VIRGINIA WOMAN
Letter (1777)

Canvas. Height 34 in.; width 29 in. (0.86 x 0.74). Painted in 1795 in Philadelphia, and known as the Vaughan Washington. It was engraved when in the collection of its first owner, Samuel Vaughan, and is generally considered the first of three portraits of Washington painted from life. From this picture Stuart made at least fifteen replicas, but in these a quality of realism that distinguishes the Vaughan canvas has been lost. Collections: Samuel Vaughan, William Vaughan, London; Joseph Harrison, Philadelphia; Thomas B. Clarke, New York. *Mellon Collection,* 1942.

GILBERT STUART · American 1755-1828

Mrs. Richard Yates

After Church this afternoon we went, still under the auspices of Mr. Davis, to call upon Mr. Stuart, the painter, an American by birth, but who spends many years of his life in England. His professional education was under West, who, you know, was also an American. Mr. Stuart has done likenesses of many English naval officers who flourished some forty or fifty years ago. With Lord St. Vincent he was on terms of very great intimacy. His conversation is extremely interesting from his acquaintance with so many eminent men. In his painting room there is an original painting he did of Washington, merely a head, the figure and drapery left unfinished. He amused us exceedingly by the account he gave us of the embarrassment at first as to how he was to get on with it, he found it such hard work to make General Washington speak on light subjects; however, he resolved to try at all hazards to make him laugh, accordingly he told him the old Joe Miller story of King James II's journey to gain popularity, in the course of which he arrived somewhere that the Mayor of the place was Baker and no speech-maker and had to be prompted, so that when his friend jogged his elbow and said, "Hold up your head and look like a man," the blundering Mayor repeated the admonition to the King. This stupid story had the desired effect, "and from that time," said Mr. Stuart, "I had him on a pivot and could manage him nicely." I was still more interested with his description of David Hume and Voltaire whom he remembers sitting together in the Stoop of Mr. Hume's house at the end of the North Bridge in Edinburgh. Mr. Stewart [*sic*] was then a little boy following his education in Edinburgh, and Mr. Hume used to call him in and converse with him as he came home from school. Mr. Stuart was the first person to set Sir Thomas Lawrence agoing when he arrived in London from Bath, quite a young man, now upwards of forty years ago. Till then Sir Thomas had occupied himself merely with little drawings in crayon, but Mr. Stuart saw at once that he was a man of genius, and overlooking the rudeness of the speech asked him abruptly what made him waste his time doing such *damned* things as these? The poor young man's abashed air reminded Mr. Stuart what a breach of politeness he had been guilty of, but the complimentary apology amply compensated for the pain occasioned by the first speech.

Margaret Hall
Letter to Jane Hunter (Oct. 14, 1827)

Canvas. Height 30¼ in.; width 25 in. (0.77 x 0.64). Painted in 1793, the year following Stuart's return to New York from Ireland, this portrait of the wife of a New York merchant is generally thought to be one of the artist's finest canvases. A copy is in the Boston Museum of Fine Arts. Collections: Dr. Isaac M. Cline, New Orleans; Thomas B. Clarke, New York. *Mellon Collection,* 1940.

JOHN CONSTABLE · BRITISH 1776-1837

Wivenhoe Park, Essex

In Art as in Literature, there are two modes by which men aim at distinction; in the one the Artist by careful application to what others have accomplished, imitates their works, or selects and combines their various beauties; in the other he seeks excellence at its primitive source NATURE. The one forms a style upon the study of pictures, and produces either imitative or eclectic art, as it has been termed; the other by a close observation of nature discovers qualities existing in her, which have never been portrayed before, and thus forms a style which is original. The results of the one mode, as they repeat that with which the eye is already familiar, are soon recognised and estimated; the advances of the Artist in a new path must necessarily be slow, for few are able to judge of that which deviates from the usual course or qualified to appreciate original studies.

JOHN CONSTABLE
Various Subjects of Landscape (1832)

It appears to me that pictures have been over-valued; held up by a blind admiration as ideal things, and almost as standards by which nature is to be judged rather than the reverse; and this false estimate has been sanctioned by the extravagant epithets that have been applied to painters, as 'the divine,' 'the inspired,' and so forth. Yet, in reality, what are the most sublime productions of the pencil but selections of some of the forms of nature, and copies of a few of her evanescent effects; and this is the result, not of inspiration, but of long and patient study, under the direction of much good sense. — It was said by Sir Thomas Lawrence, that 'we can never hope to compete with nature in the beauty and delicacy of her separate forms or colours, — our only chance lies in selection and combination.' Nothing can be more true, — and it may be added, that selection and combination are learned from nature herself, who constantly presents us with compositions of her own, far more beautiful than the happiest arranged by human skill. I have endeavoured to draw a line between genuine art and mannerism, but even the greatest painters have never been wholly untainted by manner. — Painting is a science, and should be pursued as an inquiry into the laws of nature. Why, then may not landscape painting be considered as a branch of natural philosophy, of which pictures are but the experiments?

JOHN CONSTABLE
Lectures on Landscape Painting (June 16, 1836)

Canvas. Height 21¼ in.; width 39¼ in. (0.54 x 1.00). Painted in the summer of 1816, and exhibited at the Royal Academy in 1817. Wivenhoe Park was the country seat of Major General Rebow, an old friend of Constable's father, and one of the artist's earliest patrons. In the Victoria and Albert Museum, South Kensington, are two small pencil sketches by Constable, one of Wivenhoe Park, the other of Wivenhoe Park with Church. Collections: Wivenhoe Park Collection. *Widener Collection*, 1942.

J. M. W. TURNER · BRITISH 1775-1851

Keelmen Heaving in Coals by Moonlight

No other man gives me any notion of that infinity of hues and tints and gradations of light and shade which Nature displays to those who have eyes for such sights, except Turner: no one else gives me such a sense of the power of the elements, no one else lifts up the veil and discloses the *penetralia* of Nature, as this painter does. The liquid look of his ocean and its lifesomeness . . . . are what one might look for in vain in any but the Turnerian quarter.

SARA COLERIDGE
Letter to Miss Erskine (1845)

LANDSCAPE

In this department TURNER is transcendent. He exhibits five pictures, each different from the other in subject and effect, and all resplendently beautiful. . . . "Keelmen Heaving in Coals by Night" is a view on the Tyne; on which the full moon pours a flood of silver radiance that fills the scene, excepting the dusky line of colliers, with the light and smoke of the beacons on the river-side. The aerial brilliancy of the effect is surprising. The tone seems too like daylight; but a year or two hence it will be as bright and true a night scene as ever — or rather *never* was painted. . . . TURNER paints for posterity, and allows for the effect of time, as Robin Hood when he shot allowed for the wind: and having seen the effect of TURNER's aim, we will not while his arrow is in mid-flight venture to doubt its hitting the mark.

The Spectator (1835)

ROYAL ACADEMY

Mr. Turner has several pictures. Two more particularly beyond the rest demand attention. No. 24, "Keelmen heaving in Coals, by Night," . . . . is a moonlight scene, and admirably adapted for displaying the masterly pencil of Mr. Turner. The picture is as light as day, and the only thing that prevents the impression on the mind of the spectator that it is day, is the positive coldness peculiar to moonlight. It is a most extraordinary piece of effect.

The New Monthly Magazine (1835)

Canvas. Height 36 in.; width 48 in. (0.91 x 1.22). Signed J. M. W. T. Painted for H. McConnel, of Manchester, and exhibited at the Royal Academy in 1835. Collections: This picture and a companion piece, entitled View of Venice, also in the National Gallery of Art, were sold by Mr. McConnel in 1849 to John Naylor, of Leighton Hall, Montgomeryshire, England, where they remained until they came to America. *Widener Collection*, 1942.

WILLIAM BLAKE · British 1757-1827

Queen Katherine's Dream

The great and golden rule of art, as well as of life, is this: That the more distinct, sharp, and wirey the bounding line, the more perfect the work of art; and the less keen and sharp, the greater is the evidence of weak imitation, plagiarism, and bungling. Great inventors, in all ages, knew this: Protogenes and Apelles knew each other by this line. Rafael and Michael Angelo, and Albert Durer, are known by this and this alone. The want of this determinate and bounding form evidences the want of idea in the artist's mind, and the pretence of the plagiary in all its branches. How do we distinguish the oak from the beech, the horse from the ox, but by the bounding outline? How do we distinguish one face or countenance from another, but by the bounding line and its infinite inflexions and movements? What is it that builds a house and plants a garden, but the definite and determinate? What is it that distinguishes honesty from knavery, but the hard and wiry line of rectitude and certainty in the actions and intentions. Leave out this line and you leave out life itself; all is chaos again, and the line of the almighty must be drawn out upon it before man or beast can exist.

William Blake
A Descriptive Catalogue of Pictures (1809)

The execution of my Designs, being all in Water-colours, (that is in Fresco) are regularly refused to be exhibited by the *Royal Academy,* and the *British Institution* has, this year, followed its example, and has effectually excluded me by this Resolution; I therefore invite those Noblemen and Gentleman [*sic*], who are its Subscribers, to inspect what they have excluded: and those who have been told that my Works are but an unscientific and irregular Eccentricity, a Madman's Scrawls, I demand of them to do me the justice to examine before they decide.

There cannot be more than two or three great Painters or Poets in any Age or Country; and these, in a corrupt state of Society, are easily excluded, but not so easily obstructed. They have exluded [*sic*] Water-colours; it is therefore become necessary that I should exhibit to the Public, in an Exhibition of my own, my Designs, Painted in Water-colours. If Italy is enriched and made great by Raphael, if Michael Angelo is its supreme glory, if Art is the glory of a Nation, if Genius and Inspiration are the great Origin and Bond of Society, the distinction my Works have obtained from those who best understand such things, calls for my Exhibition as the greatest of Duties to my Country.

William Blake
Exhibition of Paintings in Fresco (1809)

Paper. Height 16⅛ in.; width 13½ in. (0.41 x 0.34). Signed. This was one of two water-color drawings commissioned by Sir Thomas Lawrence, and finished by Blake just before his death in 1827. It illustrates the following passage from Shakespeare's *King Henry VIII* (Act IV, Scene II): "Enter, solemnly tripping one after another, six personages clad in white robes, wearing on their heads garlands of bays, and golden vizards on their faces; branches of bays or palm in their hands. They first congee unto her, then dance; and, at certain changes, the first two hold a spare garland over her head; at which the other four make reverent curtsies. Then the two that held the garland deliver the same to the other next two, who observe the same order in their changes and holding the garland over her head; which done, they deliver the same garland to the last two, who likewise observe the same order; at which (as it were by inspiration) she makes (in her sleep) signs of rejoicing and holdeth up her hands to heaven. And so in their dancing vanish, carrying the garland with them. *The music continues.*" Collections: Sir Thomas Lawrence, London; J. C. Strange, Professor Tylor, Mrs. Sydney Morse, London. *Lessing J. Rosenwald Collection,* 1943.

JACQUES-LOUIS DAVID · FRENCH 1748-1825

Madame Hamelin

David was not particularly original in composition. Throughout his career he was too concerned with combatting and reforming the accepted method of representation to direct his full attention to the art of developing and asserting an idea. . . . David's great merit lies in his revision of the grammar and syntax of the art of painting, which his predecessors had so strangely corrupted. He learned, first for himself, and then taught others, how to draw, to paint, and to color with truth and distinction — something no other artist had done for sixty years. As head of a school he should, therefore, be placed among the great masters; he deserves particular credit for having trained a great many able pupils, none of whom became his slavish imitator. This is praise which could perhaps be given to Raphael, but which cannot be accorded to Leonardo da Vinci and still less to the great Michelangelo.

But among these celebrated men, what rank must we assign to David as a draftsman, as an interpreter of form? Born and brought up in the middle of the eighteenth century, David, who by nature was strongly inclined toward the tender feelings and graceful fancies of the imagination, had already produced *Les Horaces* without discovering the style that was to suit his talent best. Apparently it was chance that roused him from this uncertainty and took him to Rome at the very moment when a passion for the works of antiquity, intensified by the recent discovery of the cities of Herculaneum and Pompeii, brought about the complete renovation of art. David, who until then had been drifting, with no theory to guide him or genius to create one, hastened to accept the system of archaism set forth by Winckelmann and other scholars. From that moment, he followed his chosen path with ever-increasing determination.

E. J. DELÉCLUZE
Louis David, son école et son temps (1855)

Canvas. Height 49¼ in.; width 37½ in. (1.25 x 0.95). Painted about 1800. Also known as Portrait of a Young Girl in White. The subject has been identified as Madame Hamelin, a Creole born in Santo Domingo. She became the wife of a Parisian banker, and played a brilliant role in Parisian society of the Directoire period. She was nicknamed "La Jolie Laide." Chateaubriand, whom she captivated, said of her that she possessed the two qualities that also characterized France, nobility and frivolity. Collections: H. O. Havemeyer, New York. *Chester Dale Collection*, 1941.

JEAN-BAPTISTE-CAMILLE COROT · FRENCH 1796-1875

A View Near Volterra

An ugly set of lines is not to be found in Corot; the rhythm may sometimes be weak, but his lines never run out of metre. For the rhythm of line as well as of sound the artist must seek in his own soul; he will never find it in the inchoate and discordant jumble which we call nature.

And, after all, what is art but rhythm? Corot knew that art is nature made rhythmical, and so he was never known to take out a six-foot canvas to copy nature on. Being an artist, he preferred to observe nature, and he lay down and dreamed his fields and trees, and he walked about in his landscape, selecting his point of view, determining the rhythm of his lines. That sense of rhythm which I have defined as art was remarkable in him even from his first pictures. . . .

I only saw Corot once. It was in some woods near Paris, where I had gone to paint, and I came across the old gentleman unexpectedly, seated in front of his easel in a pleasant glade. After admiring his work I ventured to say: "Master, what you are doing is lovely, but I cannot find your composition in the landscape before us." He said: "My foreground is a long way ahead," and sure enough, nearly two hundred yards away, his picture rose out of the dimness of the dell, stretching a little beyond the vista into the meadow.

The anecdote seems to me to be a real lesson in the art of painting, for it shows us the painter in his very employment of nature, and we divine easily the transposition in the tones and in the aspect of things that he was engaged in bringing into that picture. . . .

Corot and Rembrandt, as Dutilleux pointed out, arrived at the same goal by absolutely different ends. He saw clearly, although he could not express himself quite clearly, that, above all painters, Rembrandt and Corot excelled in that mode of pictorial expression known as values, or shall I say chiaroscuro, for in truth he who has said values has hinted chiaroscuro. Rembrandt told all that a golden ray falling through a darkened room awakens in a visionary brain; Corot told all that the grey light of morning and evening whispers in the pensive mind of the elegiac poet. The story told was widely different, but the manner of telling was the same: one attenuated in the light, the other attenuated in the shadow: both sacrificed the corners with a view to fixing the attention on the one spot in which the soul of the picture lives.

GEORGE MOORE
Modern Painting (1893)

Canvas. Height 27¼ in.; width 37¼ in. (0.69 x 0.95). Signed, and dated 1838. According to recent critics, this picture was exhibited at the Salon of 1838, under the title Vue Prise à Volterra, though Robaut tentatively suggests that the picture shown at the Salon that year was another version, also dated 1838. In either event, the present picture is based on studies done in 1834, at the time of Corot's visit to Volterra, during his second Italian journey. Collections: Baronne Thénard, Paris. *Chester Dale Collection, 1941.*

JEAN-BAPTISTE-CAMILLE COROT · French 1796-1875

Agostina

Corot, preoccupied at first with sheer craftsmanship, applied himself to the problem of capturing rapidly, in specific studies, a silhouette, a type, a costume. The tenderness of his affections prompted him to set down the features of his friends and his family; historical landscape drew his attention to the stylization of the figures; finally, one fine day, he is moved by the human figure. From that time it ceases to be purely an object of study, it becomes a fundamental impetus. . . . Those realistic figures are frank, living, rigorously studied, more agreeable than all the others. But suddenly overcome again by an inward vision, Corot envelops, caresses, softens all that is too brutal in real life, creating those figures which are so poetic, so delicate, so subtle that they seem immaterial, hardly of this world.

It is woman almost exclusively that attracts Corot's brush, and he, so little intellectual, so little sophisticated, represents her as an enigma, a problem to be solved. It is a problem that he reconsiders untiringly, apparently without ever discovering the solution. Thus, this old bachelor represented woman now as an ideal dream, impossible of realization, now as an overwhelming reality, better fitted to deceive than to charm.

Not one is gay. Their faces are stern and inscrutable. When they are young, a gentle melancholy suffuses their features; grown old, they recall what Fromentin wrote of Memling's portraits: "One finds in them something solemn and experienced, which gives them the air of having passed their lives in suffering, and in reflecting upon their sorrows." Is this not the exact definition of the countenance of the woman in blue? A few of his works escape the fatality that seems to weigh upon these heads. These are the mothers with their children, some portraits and a few canvases from which radiates, if not joy, at least a gentle gladness.

The moral significance of these faces is striking, surprising and extremely fascinating, but might this not be simply a reflection of the spirit of the time? Corot's women dream gravely, sadly, just as portraits by Latour or busts by Houdon smile with an unconscious levity, a spontaneous grace which is the very soul of the eighteenth century.

C. Bernheim de Villers
Corot, peintre de figures (1930)

Canvas. Height 51¼ in.; width 37½ in. (1.30 x 0.95). Signed. Painted probably in 1866. This date, first suggested by Robaut, is based on the fact that Lavieille, one of Corot's pupils, used the same model in a painting inscribed, "In the studio of M. Corot, February, 1866." The present painting, reminiscent of Italian landscape and costume, was actually executed many years after Corot's last Italian journey. Collections: Breysse, Faure, Paton, Bernheim-Jeune, Paris. *Chester Dale Collection*, 1941.

HONORE DAUMIER · French 1808-1879

Advice to a Young Artist

Now I should like to speak of one of our most important men, not only in caricature but also in modern art, a man who, every morning, entertains the people of Paris, and who, each day, satisfies and nourishes the need for public amusement. The bourgeois, the businessman, the urchin, the housewife all laugh at his pictures, though often — ungrateful wretches — they overlook his name. So far, only artists have realized that there is earnestness in his work, and that it is really worthy of study. You will have guessed that I am speaking of Daumier. . . .

Daumier is a great caricaturist, with a highly developed and serious art. To appreciate him properly, one must analyze him from an artistic and from an ethical point of view. As an artist, Daumier is distinguished by his assurance. He draws like the great masters. His drawing is broad, facile, a constant improvisation yet never divorced from reality. He has a marvelous, almost super-human memory, which serves him in place of a model. All his figures are well poised, always convincing in their movement. His gift of observation is so sure that one finds in his work not a single head unsuited to the body that supports it. . . .

Ethically, Daumier bears some relation to Molière. Like him, he goes straight to the point. His idea is immediately defined; one can understand it at a glance. The captions beneath his drawings are of little consequence, for they generally could be omitted. His humor is, so to speak, involuntary. Rather than being sought by the artist, an idea seems to escape from him spontaneously. His caricature is exceedingly broad, but without malice or venom. There is a fundamental fairness and good nature in all his work. Often — and this is an important characteristic — he has refused to satirize an exceptionally fine or intense subject, on the grounds that he might overstep the limits of comedy or offend the feelings of the public. Furthermore, when he is heart-rending or terrifying, it is unintentional, the result of his depicting some hing he has seen. Because he loves life so passionately and so unaffectedly, it would be difficult for him to turn to pure comedy. He carefully avoids anything not clearly and immediately perceptible to a French audience.

CHARLES BAUDELAIRE
Curiosités esthétiques (1868)

Canvas. Height 16 in.; width 13 in. (0.41 x 0.33). Painted probably after 1860. The present canvas was perhaps a gift from Daumier to his close friend and benefactor, Corot, in whose collection it is first recorded. It was shown at the great retrospective exhibition of Daumier's work in 1901, at the Ecole des Beaux-Arts, Paris. Collections: J.-B.-C. Corot, Adolphe A. Tavernier, Paris. *Gift of Duncan Phillips,* 1941.

EDOUARD MANET · French 1832-1883

The Old Musician

At first a canvas by Manet gives a rather harsh impression. One is not accustomed to seeing such simple and sincere translations of reality. Furthermore, as I have said, there is a certain elegant inflexibility which is surprising. At first the eye sees only colors, broadly laid on. Soon, the objects take form and fall into their places; at the end of a few seconds, the whole composition stands out boldly, and one takes genuine delight in contemplating this lucid and serious painting, which represents nature with a gentle brutality, if I may use such an expression. Coming closer to the picture, one sees that the handling is delicate rather than abrupt; the artist uses only his brush, and uses it with prudence: there is no piling up of colors, but an even coat. The methods of this bold painter, who has been made fun of, are exceedingly sound, and if his works look strange, it is only because of the extremely personal way in which he perceives objects and interprets them.

In short, were I questioned, were I asked what new language Edouard Manet speaks, I should answer: he speaks a language of simplicity and precision. His keynote is that blond tone which fills the canvas with light. The translation he gives us is an accurate and simplified translation, proceeding by generalities, indicating only the main masses.

We must, I cannot too often repeat, forget thousands of things in order to understand and to enjoy this talent. There is no longer question of a search for absolute beauty; the artist is not painting history or the soul; what is known as composition does not exist for him, and the task he sets himself is not the representation of such-and-such an idea or of such-and-such an historical action. And that is why he must not be judged as a moralist or a man of letters; he must be judged as a painter. He handles figure paintings in the manner considered suitable by the academies for the treatment of still life; I mean that he groups the figures before him, rather casually, and that thereafter his only concern is to set them down on his canvas as he sees them, with the strong contrasts they make as one stands out from the other. Do not ask of him anything but a correct, literal translation. He would not know how to sing or to philosophize. He knows how to paint, and that is that. He has the gift, and this is his particular bent, of perceiving the niceties of the main tones, and thus of being able to model objects and human beings in broad planes.

EMILE ZOLA
Edouard Manet (1867)

Canvas. Height 73¾ in.; width 98 in. (1.88 x 2.49). Signed, and dated 1862. Also known as The Wandering Musician. A drawing of the painting is listed by P. Jamot and G. Wildenstein (*Manet*). The little girl holding the baby appears in an etching by Manet, and the cloaked figure at the right is from his painting of 1859 entitled The Absinthe Drinker. In the arrangement of the figures, the painting shows the influence of Velázquez' Los Borrachos, which Manet knew through reproductions, possibly Goya's famous plate. Collections: The Manet Family, Paris; Prince de Wagram, Paris; P. R. Pearson, Paris; Imperial Museum, Vienna; C. C. Hodebert, Paris. *Chester Dale Collection*, 1941.

JAMES A. McNEILL WHISTLER · AMERICAN 1834-1903

The White Girl

Whistler gives you the picture, then, frankly as a picture. He gives it to you for its lines, its colours, as at all events its primary meaning for him; a meaning in itself almost or quite sufficient, if need be, but capable of an indefinite extension or deepening. Unlike most men, he sees, sees really, with a complete indifference to what other significance things may have, besides their visible aspect.

Only, for him, the visible aspect of things is the aspect of a continual miracle, and it is from this fresh sense of wonder that there comes that mystery in which he envelops mere flesh and blood, in which there is no inherent strangeness. Some aspect of a thing dreamed or seen in passing, and then remembered in the transfiguring memory of the brain, comes hauntingly into all his faces. The look they show you is not the look which their mirror sees every morning and every evening. It has come to them out of the eye that sees them, as it were, for the first time. Until Whistler looked at this young girl's face, it was but a young girl's face; now it is something besides, it means all that the brush has thought into it, it has the weight and meaning and mysterious questioning of a work of art. Every work of art is an interrogation; these faces exist softly, like flowers, delicately on a canvas; they challenge us idly, offering their most secret perfumes if we will but drink them in. They await time in an uneager patience, content to be themselves. They have the flower's assurance, the flower's humility.

Look round a picture gallery, and you will recognise a Whistler at once, and for this reason first, that it does not come to meet you. Most of the other pictures seem to cry across the floor: 'Come and look at us, see how like something we are!' Their voices cross and jangle like the voices of rival sellers in a street fair. Each out-bids his neighbour, promising you more than your money's worth. The Whistlers smile secretly in their corner, and say nothing. They are not really indifferent; they watch and wait, and when you come near them they seem to efface themselves, as if they would not have you even see them too closely. That is all part of the subtle malice with which they win you. They choose you, you do not choose them. . . .

It is significant of a certain simplicity in his attitude towards his own work, that Whistler, in all his fighting on behalf of principles, has never tried to do more than establish (shall I say?) the correctness of his grammar. He has never asked for more praise than should be the reward of every craftsman who is not a bungler. He has claimed that, setting out to do certain things, legitimate in themselves, he has done them in a way legitimate in itself. All the rest he is content to leave out of the question: that is to say, everything but a few primary qualities, without which no one can, properly speaking, be a painter at all.

ARTHUR SYMONS
Studies in Seven Arts (1906)

Canvas. Height 85½ in.; width 43 in. (2.17 x 1.09). Signed, and dated 1862. The model was Joanna Heffernan, a famous beauty who also posed for Courbet. The painting was exhibited at the Salon des Refusés of 1863, along with Manet's Déjeuner sur l'Herbe and other paintings rejected by the jury of the regular Salon. Collections: *Harris Whittemore Collection*, 1943.

EDGAR DEGAS · FRENCH 1834-1917

Achille de Gas in the Uniform of a Cadet

Degas rejected *facility* just as he rejected everything that was not the sole object of his thoughts. He desired only his own approval, that is to say, to satisfy the most exigent, the harshest and most incorruptible of judges. No one more positively scorned honors, advantages, riches, and that glory which the writer can dispense to the artist so easily and with such generous heedlessness. He scathingly jeered those who put the fate of their work at the mercy of public opinion, of the established powers, or of commercial interests. As the true believer is concerned only with God, in whose sight all subterfuges, all deceits, all compromises or connivance, either of attitudes or appearances, count as naught, so he remained intact and unchanging, subject only to the absolute idea which he held of his art. He wanted only that which he found most difficult to exact of himself. . . .

Despite the fact that he was born when "Romanticism" was at its height, that, about the time of his maturity, he perforce joined the "Naturalist" movement, consorted with Duranty, Zola, Goncourt, Duret, and exhibited with the first "Impressionists", he remained, nevertheless, one of those delightful *connoisseurs* — obstinately, voluptuously narrow, merciless toward novelties which have nothing but their novelty to recommend them, nourished by Racine and early music, given to quotations, classicist to the point of violence, extravagance and brilliance — unfortunately a vanished type nowadays. . . .

A man of taste, Degas was out of step with his times in this respect while by the genuine boldness and precision of his thought, he was far ahead of many of his artist contemporaries. He was one of the first to understand what the painter could learn from photography and what the painter must beware of borrowing from it. . . .

After long examination, all the arts deepen into insoluble problems. The prolonged gaze engenders infinite difficulties, and this creation of imaginary obstacles, of conflicting desires, of scruples and regrets, is proportionate, or even more than proportionate, to one's intelligence and one's knowledge. How can one choose sides between Raphael and the Venetians, sacrifice Mozart to Wagner, Shakespeare to Racine? These perplexities hold nothing tragic for the amateur or the critic. For the artist they are pangs of conscience, renewed each time that he re-examines the work he has completed.

Degas finds himself caught between the precepts of Ingres and the strange fascination of Delacroix; while he hesitates, the art of his time decides to exploit the contemporary scene. Compositions in the Grand Manner become outmoded. Landscape invades the walls abandoned by the Greeks and the Turks, the Knights and the Cupids. It destroys the notion of *subject matter* and, in only a few years, reduces all the intellectual side of art to a few discussions about *matter* and the color of shadows. The mind becomes purely a retina and there can no longer be any question of trying, by one's brush, to express the feelings of some old men before a lovely Suzanna or the noble resistance of a great physician to whom millions are offered.

PAUL VALÉRY
Degas Danse Dessin (1938)

Canvas. Height 25¼ in.; width 20 in. (0.64 x 0.51). Painted c. 1856. Like most of the family portraits by Degas, this portrait of his brother as a naval cadet remained in the possession of the family until recently. Collections: René de Gas, Paris. *Chester Dale Collection*, 1941.

HENRI FANTIN-LATOUR · FRENCH 1836-1904

Still Life

Fantin's talent is seen at its best in his still-lives, for in these simple compositions, often so quaintly arranged, he develops a style that is distinctly his own. . . .

To describe one of his still-lives is to describe many of them; there are dozens which differ scarcely at all in general effect. One who has seen many of his canvases in various private collections, carries away the impression that they are quite uniform in style. For what he does is simply to paint a bouquet of flowers, of various kinds, in a vase against a grey background. . . .

Descriptions like these do not indicate the charm which the pictures actually possess; tightly bunched bouquets of red, pink and blue do not suggest decoration nor much originality in arrangement. But it must be remembered that against a neutral background almost any color scheme will work. That is why a Fantin is never crude. No matter how exciting the motley of red and pink and purple may appear, the surrounding grey gives rest. So that his vase of flowers is like a rich jewel against the velvet of a woman's dress, or a stained glass window within the gloom of a cathedral. The flowers are as vibrant sparkles of light out of the sombreness of a dull sky. This is the secret of Fantin-Latour, and this is why Geffroy could write, "The smallest canvas of Fantin-Latour is a scheme where nothing is lacking to constitute a definite decoration."

But more must be said. Within the burst of splendor there is far more refinement, arrangement, display of taste than is at first apparent. The colors will appear to arrange themselves so that the whites, the salmons and the pinks of roses will group together, forming a conspicuous mass and the chief point of interest in the picture. The warmest tones, the reds, the yellows, and the oranges will be nearest the centre; and, as the bouquet curves around and over, the violets and the blues will be found. Separating them yet unifying them, are the green leaves. These colors, therefore, have not fallen so, like bits of sparkle in a kaleidoscope, but they were placed so by a luminist who understood the rules of color vibration and of harmony. And it is apparent that this is the new colorism — not that of the old masters — but of Manet, cool, bright, pure and lustrous, enveloped not in shadow, but in a clear atmosphere and light. Nevertheless there is no impressionism in his handling; every flower is carefully studied. Its individual form and texture is preserved yet not too detailed to destroy its freshness. For this reason Fantin's flowers are more satisfactory than Manet's.

ARTHUR EDWIN BYE
Pots and Pans (1921)

Canvas. Height 23¼ in.; width 28¾ in. (0.59 x 0.73). Signed, and dated 1866. In this year Fantin seems to have painted nothing but still life. Whistler, who had studied with Fantin in Bovin's studio in Paris under the direction of Courbet, introduced Fantin's work to England, and it was there that most of Fantin's still-life paintings found enthusiastic collectors. Collections: Reginald Davis, A. T. Hollingsworth, London. *Chester Dale Collection*, 1941.

AUGUSTE RENOIR · FRENCH 1841-1919

Odalisque

Renoir: I can give you a personal example of influences in painting. At the beginning, I used to put paint on thick, thinking I would get more "value" that way. One day, at the Louvre, I noticed that Rubens had obtained more by a simple rubbing than I did with all my heavy layers. Another time, I discovered that Rubens produced a silver with black. I learned my lesson, of course; but does that necessarily mean that I was influenced by Rubens?

Vollard: (I began to ask myself if all the things which had impressed me so much were not simply "literature." I made one last try:)

At any rate, the Impressionists excel in "painting by chance sensations and by the powerful clairvoyance of instinct. . . ."

Renoir (interrupting): "Chance sensations"! "Power of the instincts"! Like the animals, eh? That sounds like the fools who congratulate us on giving our models "expressive poses." Those good people do not realize that Cézanne called his compositions souvenirs of the museums; for my part, I have always tried to paint human beings just as I would beautiful fruit. Look at the greatest of modern painters, Corot, and see if his women are "thinkers." But if you try to tell those people that the most important thing for a painter is to know good colours, just as the mason ought to know the best mortar — And the first Impressionists worked away without ever even thinking of a sale! It is the only thing our imitators have forgotten to copy. . . .

The truth is that in painting, as in the other arts, there's not a single process, no matter how insignificant, which can reasonably be made into a formula. For instance, I tried long ago to measure out, once and for all, the amount of oil which I put in my colour. I simply could not do it. I have to judge the amount necessary with each dip of the brush. The "scientific" artists thought they had discovered a truth once they had learned that the juxtaposition of yellow and blue gives violet shadows. But even when you know that, you still don't know anything. There is something in painting which cannot be explained, and that something is the essential. You come to Nature with your theories, and she knocks them all flat. . . .

The popularization of art, indeed! That's enough to make you give it all up! Fortunately there is no stupidity in the world that can make a painter stop painting.

AMBROISE VOLLARD
Auguste Renoir (1920)

Canvas. Height 27 in.; width 48½ in. (0.69 x 1.23). Signed, and dated 1870. Also known as L'Orientale. This painting gives striking evidence of the artist's admiration for the style of Delacroix, whose exotic Femmes d'Alger he was copying at about this time. Collections: Hugo Perls, Berlin; G. F. Reber, Lausanne. *Chester Dale Collection,* 1941.

AUGUSTE RENOIR · FRENCH 1841-1919

A Girl with a Watering Can

What, then, is so peculiar about Renoir is that he has this perfectly ordinary taste in things and yet remains so intensely, so purely, an artist. The fact is perhaps that he was so much an artist that he never had to go round the corner to get his inspiration; the immediate, obvious, front view of everything was more than sufficient to start the creative impulse. He enjoyed instinctively, almost animally, all the common good things of life, and yet he always kept just enough detachment to feel his delight æsthetically — he kept, as it were, just out of reach of appetite.

More than any other great modern artist Renoir trusted implicitly to his own sensibility; he imposed no barrier between his own delight in certain things and the delight which he communicates. He liked passionately the obviously good things of life, the young human animal, sunshine, sky, trees, water, fruit; the things that every one likes; only he liked them at just the right distance with just enough detachment to replace appetite by emotion. He could rely on this detachment so thoroughly that he could dare, what hardly any other genuine modern has dared to say how much he liked even a pretty sight. But what gives his art so immediate, so universal an appeal is that his detachment went no further than was just necessary. His sensibility is kept at the exact point where it is transmuted into emotion. And the emotion, though it has of course the generalised æsthetic feeling, keeps something of the fulness and immediacy of the simpler attitude. Not that Renoir was either naïve or stupid. When he chose he showed that he was capable of logical construction and vigorous design. But for his own pleasure he would, as he himself said, have been satisfied to make little isolated records of his delight in the detail of a flower or a lock of hair. . . .

The first approach to one of his pictures may indeed remind one of pictures that would be the delight of the servants' hall, so unaffectedly simple is his acceptance of the charm of rosy-cheeked girls, of pretty posies and dappled sunlight. And yet one knows well enough that Renoir was as "artful" as one could wish. Though he had not the biting wit of a Degas, he had a peculiar love of mischievous humour; he was anything but a harmless or innocent character. All his simplicity is on the surface only. The longer one looks, the deeper does Renoir retire behind veil after veil of subtlety. And yet, compared with some modern artists, he was, after all, easy and instinctively simple.

ROGER FRY
Vision and Design (1920)

Canvas. Height 39½ in.; width 28¾ in. (1.00 x 0.73). Signed and dated 1876. The intimate charm of the subject, the way in which figure and landscape are fused, the use of flat color patterns, that characterize this and other Renoir paintings of the same period, form the basis of the style developed by such later *Intimistes* as Bonnard and Vuillard. Collections: Paul Bérard, Paris; A. Rosenberg, Paris; Prince de Wagram, Paris. *Chester Dale Collection*, 1941.

The Loge

I would almost rather see you dead!

ROBERT S. CASSATT

To his daughter Mary when she left Pittsburgh to study art in Paris (1868)

Let us suppose that a father from the highest motives did not wish his daughter to leave home and become writer, painter or scholar. "See what Mr. Oscar Browning says," he would say; and there was not only Mr. Oscar Browning; there was the *Saturday Review;* there was Mr. Greg — the "essentials of a woman's being," said Mr. Greg emphatically, "are that *they are supported by, and they minister to, men*" — there was an enormous body of masculine opinion to the effect that nothing could be expected of women intellectually. Even if her father did not read out loud these opinions, any girl could read them for herself; and the reading, even in the nineteenth century, must have lowered her vitality, and told profoundly upon her work. There would always have been that assertion — you cannot do this, you are incapable of doing that — to protest against, to overcome. Probably for a novelist this germ is no longer of much effect; for there have been women novelists of merit. But for painters it must still have some sting in it; and for musicians, I imagine, is even now active and poisonous in the extreme. The woman composer stands where the actress stood in the time of Shakespeare. Nick Greene, I thought, remembering the story I had made about Shakespeare's sister, said that a woman acting put him in mind of a dog dancing. Johnson repeated the phrase two hundred years later of women preaching. And here, I said, opening a book about music, we have the very words used again in this year of grace, 1928, of women who try to write music. "Of Mlle. Germaine Tailleferre one can only repeat Dr. Johnson's dictum concerning a woman preacher, transposed into terms of music. 'Sir, a woman's composing is like a dog's walking on his hind legs. It is not done well, but you are surprised to find it done at all.' " So accurately does history repeat itself.

Thus, I concluded, shutting Mr. Oscar Browning's life and pushing away the rest, it is fairly evident that even in the nineteenth century a woman was not encouraged to be an artist. On the contrary, she was snubbed, slapped, lectured and exhorted. Her mind must have been strained and her vitality lowered by the need of opposing this, of disproving that. For here again we come within range of that very interesting and obscure masculine complex which has had so much influence upon the woman's movement; that deep-seated desire, not so much that *she* shall be inferior as that *he* shall be superior, which plants him wherever one looks, not only in front of the arts, but barring the way to politics too, even when the risk to himself seems infinitesimal and the suppliant humble and devoted.

VIRGINIA WOOLF

A Room of One's Own (1929)

Canvas. Height 31½ in.; width 25¼ in. (0.80 x 0.64). Signed. Painted about 1882. The delicacy of color and sensitiveness of interpretation in this double portrait are characteristic of Mary Cassatt's early style, which was strongly influenced by the technique and the subject matter of the French Impressionists. The use of a box at the theater as a setting appears as a recurring motif in a number of the artist's works, including a preliminary drawing for The Loge, also in the Chester Dale Collection, National Gallery of Art. Collections: Baron Herzog, Budapest; Marczell von Nemes, Budapest. *Chester Dale Collection,* 1942.

WINSLOW HOMER · American 1836-1910

Breezing Up

Homer's subject-matter was the most romantic possible. Romantic because it told romantic stories, not the word-picture stories of Delacroix, of historical romanticism, Walter Scott and Hugo; nor the stories of the British painters that came on butcher calendars; not the stories of Dickens or Stevenson, but the stories one feels that one has written, because Thoreau or Burroughs or even Ernest Seton Thompson said that one knew so. The stories of the camp fire and the tiller, the stories of sailing and hunting of the woods, the sea stories where women take small part, like the world's best stories, for good stories deal not with facts but with ideas. . . .

From his fortieth to his seventy-fourth year, Homer never relapsed into formula, although he constantly reworked the same subjects. His drawings are calligraphic; they are never typographical. The formulas of magazine drafting which he employed as an illustrator are used not so much as short cuts for himself as short cuts for those who look at his pictures. All his pictures are addressed not only to the senses but to the intelligence through the senses. The science he teaches, the intrinsic relationship between objects and forces, could not have been conveyed by the pseudo-scientific methods of the impressionism of his time, for this impressionism was concerned more with atmosphere than with objects. . . . Homer's interest lay in how much one can see by night, or storm of rain or snow or mist, rather than in how faintly we see things under these circumstances. He understood that obscurity is not mystery. While the impressionists thought only of the sensations which objects give us, Homer always kept the object itself in his mind. He gives us not merely its appearance; he not only gives us the object but tells us about it by leading us into it. His time of day, his light, which is that with least play of shadow, with least atmosphere, is chosen and contrived for this purpose. . . . His favorite hours are those with least nuance, broad noon sun or dark night, an overcast bleak sky. The light he chose, under which one must paint well in order to paint anything, drove him to draw and render rather better than he knew how.

John Wheelwright
Remington and Winslow Homer
Hound & Horn (1933)

Canvas. Height 24 in.; width 38 in. (0.61 x 0.97). Signed, and dated 1876. Apparently Homer began this painting in 1873, for in writing to a prospective purchaser in 1876, when the painting was shown in the National Academy Exhibition, he stated that it represented three years' work. There is a water color of this subject, dated 1874, owned by the Estate of Mrs. Charles S. Homer, and a small oil, dated the same year, in the Harold T. Pulsifer Collection. Collections: Charles Stewart Smith, New York; Howard Caswell Smith, Oyster Bay, New York. *Gift of the W. L. and May T. Mellon Foundation,* 1943.

Boulevard Montmartre

Born in the Islands, where the sun warms and gilds all things, where the eyes of men, like their garments and their skin, take on torrid reflections, Camille Pissarro loved, above all, the blues, violets and greens of our Norman and Ile-de-France countryside. One may distinguish the successive periods of his production, analyze the influences which he undergoes — Corot or Cézanne, Seurat or perhaps, most recently, Luce. What has not changed is his taste for the moist tones of our climate. Whether he paints the harbors of Rouen at noon or the Avenue de l'Opéra in midsummer, and above all when some pretext is furnished by his subject (our damp meadows, the snow, our fogs), he seems to refuse to translate the brilliance of the sun by yellow and orange tones, as the theories of color he professes would demand. Thus the light of the sun has a chalky whiteness, milky amid the violet shadows, and the meadows shine green among the steel-blue coppices. His warm glance, shadowy and golden, in his dusky face — Hebraic, Spanish, Creole — took pleasure in reflecting the pale azure of our sky.

It is because he loved our countryside and its light that he was an Impressionist, and even the appellation of *plein-airiste* would have been appropriate for him, I think; since of all the discoveries of the school one alone held his heart, that of the sun! He willingly forgot that Rousseau, Millet and even Corot had painted the sun. I spoke to him one day of Claude Lorrain, but it was of sunsets that we talked! What surprised him more was what I told him about a primitive in the Museum of Siena (Giovanni di Paolo) who, in order to express the sun-drenched desert, had painted some palm trees with their shadows projected on the gold background. The sun of Pissarro was not that of the Sienese primitive, it was a pale and discreet light, filtered through the moist atmosphere of the Seine. . . .

The free, supple technique of Impressionism allowed Monet, Renoir and Berthe Morisot to glorify beautiful, pure colors and to create in light, sparkling harmonies, as though all nature were rejoicing. As for Pissarro, it was the grays that he sought out and achieved at the price of more sophisticated combinations of colors. He divided in order to neutralize. His landscapes of Vexin make one think of faded tapestries. From our most radiant sunshine, he created "Verdures". . . .

Neither lyric nor vulgar, he undertook to construct by masses and by values, solidly, those figures and rustic scenes whose opaque but delicately graded greens recapture the gracious benevolence of the valley of the Seine.

Maurice Denis
Théories (1903)

Canvas. Height 28¾ in.; width 36¼ in. (0.73 x 0.92). Signed, and dated 1897. Another painting of the Boulevard Montmartre is in the Edward G. Robinson Collection, Beverly Hills, California. It shows the same scene in the afternoon, rather than in the morning light. Painted the same year, the two pictures were probably conceived as pendants. Collections: Lessing, Berlin. *Chester Dale Collection*, 1941.

VINCENT VAN GOGH · Dutch 1853-1890

La Mousmé

29 July, 1888

You ought, if you can, to make me feel that art is living, you who love art perhaps more than I do. I tell myself that that depends not on art but on myself, that the only way to get back my confidence and peace of mind is to *do better*.

And there we are again, back at the end of my last letter — I am getting old, it's sheer imagination if I should think that art is old lumber too. And now, if you know what a "mousmé" is (you will know when you have read Loti's *Madame Chrysanthème*), I have just painted one.

It took me the whole of the week, I have not been able to do anything else, not having been very well either. That is what annoys me, if I had been well, I should have slashed at some landscapes in between times, but to do the Mousmé well I had to reserve my mental energy. A Mousmé is a Japanese girl — Provençal in this case — 12 to 14 years old. . . .

The portrait of the girl is against a background of white strongly tinged with malachite green, her bodice is striped blood red and violet, the skirt is royal blue, with broad stippling of yellow orange. The flat flesh tones are yellowish grey, the hair tinged with violet, the eyebrows are black and the eyelashes, the eyes orange and prussian blue. A branch of oleander in her fingers, for the two hands are shown.

September, 1888

If we study Japanese art, you see a man who is undoubtedly wise, philosophic and intelligent, who spends his time how? In studying the distance between the earth and the moon? No. In studying the policy of Bismarck? No. He studies a single blade of grass.

But this blade of grass leads him to draw every plant and then the seasons, the wide aspects of the countryside, then animals, then the human figure. So he passes his life, and life is too short to do the whole. . . .

I envy the Japanese the extreme clearness which everything has in their work. It never is wearisome, and never seems to be done too hurriedly. Their work is as simple as breathing, and they do a figure in a few sure strokes with the same ease as if it were as simple as buttoning your coat.

VINCENT VAN GOGH
Further Letters of Vincent van Gogh to His Brother (1929)

Canvas. Height 28¾ in.; width 23¾ in. (0.73 x 0.60). Painted July, 1888. Van Gogh was then passing through a period of enthusiasm for Japanese art, stimulated by his brother Theo's purchase of Japanese prints, and Loti's novel. A drawing in red ink for the painting is in the Museum of Fine Arts, Moscow. Collections: Mme. J. van Gogh-Bonger, C. M. van Gogh, Amsterdam; Carl Sternheim, La Hulpe, Belgium; Alphonse Kann, St. Germain-en-Laye, France; J. B. Stang, Oslo. *Chester Dale Collection*, 1942.

VINCENT VAN GOGH · Dutch 1853-1890

Self-Portrait

September, 1889

They say — and I am very willing to believe it — that it is difficult to know yourself — but it isn't easy either to paint yourself.

I am working on two portraits of myself at this moment — for lack of another model — because it is more than time I did a little figure work. One I began the day I got up, I was thin, and pale as a ghost. It is dark violet-blue and the head whitish with yellow hair, so it has a colour effect. . . .

My dear brother — it is always in between my work that I write to you — I am working like one actually possessed, more than ever I am in a dumb fury of work. And I think that this will help to cure me. Perhaps something will happen to me like what Eug. Delacroix spoke of, "I discovered painting when I had no longer teeth or breath," in the sense that my unhappy illness makes me work with a dumb fury — very slowly — but from morning till night without slackening — and — the secret is probably here — work long and slowly. . . .

Now my thoughts come in order and I feel perfectly normal, and if I think over my condition now with the hope of having as a rule between the attacks — if unfortunately it is to be feared that they will always return from time to time — of having at times periods of clearness and of work, if I think over my condition now, then really I tell myself that I must not get a fixed idea of being an invalid. But that I must continue firmly on my poor career as a painter. And so to remain from now on for good in an asylum would probably be to aggravate things. . . .

And altogether I would *rather* have a downright illness like this, than to be as I was in Paris while this was brewing.

And you will see this when you put the portrait with the light background that I have just finished, beside those that I made of myself in Paris, and that *now* I look more sane than then, even much more so.

I am even inclined to think that the portrait will tell you better than my letter how I am and that it will reassure you — it cost me some trouble to do.

VINCENT VAN GOGH
Further Letters of Vincent van Gogh to His Brother (1929)

Canvas. Height 23¼ in.; width 19 in. (0.59 x 0.48). Painted September, 1889, at St. Rémy. Letters by the artist to his brother Theo in September, 1889, describe his progress with this portrait, and with another begun at the same time. During this period, Vincent was under treatment for a mental illness in the sanitarium at St. Rémy. Collections: Mme. J. van Gogh-Bonger, Amsterdam. *Chester Dale Collection,* 1942.

PAUL CEZANNE · FRENCH 1839-1906

Still Life

The most interesting figure in modern art, and the only really interesting figure, is Cézanne: and that not so much because of his achievement as because of his struggle. . . .

There was . . . . a certain discrepancy between Cézanne's *notion* of what he wanted to produce, and his other, intuitive knowledge of what he *could* produce. For whereas the mind works in possibilities, the intuitions work in actualities, and what you *intuitively* desire, that is possible to you. Whereas what you mentally or "consciously" desire is nine times out of ten impossible: hitch your wagon to a star, and you'll just stay where you are.

So the conflict, as usual, was not between the artist and his medium, but between the artist's *mind* and the artist's *intuition* and *instinct*. And what Cézanne had to learn was not humility — cant word! — but honesty, honesty with himself. It was not a question of any gift of significant form or æsthetic ecstasy: it was a question of Cézanne being himself, just Cézanne. And when Cézanne is himself he is not Tintoretto, nor Veronese, nor anything baroque at all. Yet he is something *physical,* and even sensual: qualities which he had identified with the masters of virtuosity. . . .

Where Cézanne did sometimes escape the cliché altogether and really give a complete intuitive interpretation of actual objects is in some of the still-life compositions. To me these good still-life scenes are purely representative and quite true-to-life. Here Cézanne did what he wanted to do: he made the things quite real, he didn't deliberately leave anything out, and yet he gave us a triumphant and rich intuitive vision of a few apples and kitchen pots. For once his intuitive consciousness triumphed, and broke into utterance. And here he is inimitable. His imitators imitate his accessories of tablecloths folded like tin, etc. — the unreal parts of his pictures — but they don't imitate the pots and apples, because they can't. It's the real appleyness, and you can't imitate it. Every man must create it new and different out of himself: new and different. The moment it looks "like" Cézanne it is nothing.

·　　　·　　　·　　　·

After a fight tooth-and-nail for forty years, he did succeed in knowing an apple, fully; and, not quite so fully, a jug or two. That was all he achieved.

It seems little, and he died embittered. But it is the first step that counts, and Cézanne's apple is a great deal, more than Plato's Idea. Cézanne's apple rolled the stone from the mouth of the tomb, and if poor Cézanne couldn't unwind himself from his cerements and mental winding-sheet, but had to lie still in the tomb, till he died, still he gave us a chance.

D. H. LAWRENCE
The Paintings of D. H. Lawrence (1929)

Canvas. Height 25½ in.; width 31½ in. (0.65 x 0.80). Painted between 1890 and 1894. This canvas, also known as La Bouteille de Peppermint, is one of the most completely rendered of Cézanne's still-life paintings. The irresistible movement reminiscent of seventeenth-century design, which Cézanne achieved in his late style, is carried across the picture by a sequence of curving lines, suggested in the pattern and the folds of tablecloth and napkin. Collections: Ambroise Vollard, Paris; Maurice Gangnat, Paris; Emile Staub, Zurich, Switzerland. *Chester Dale Collection*, 1941.

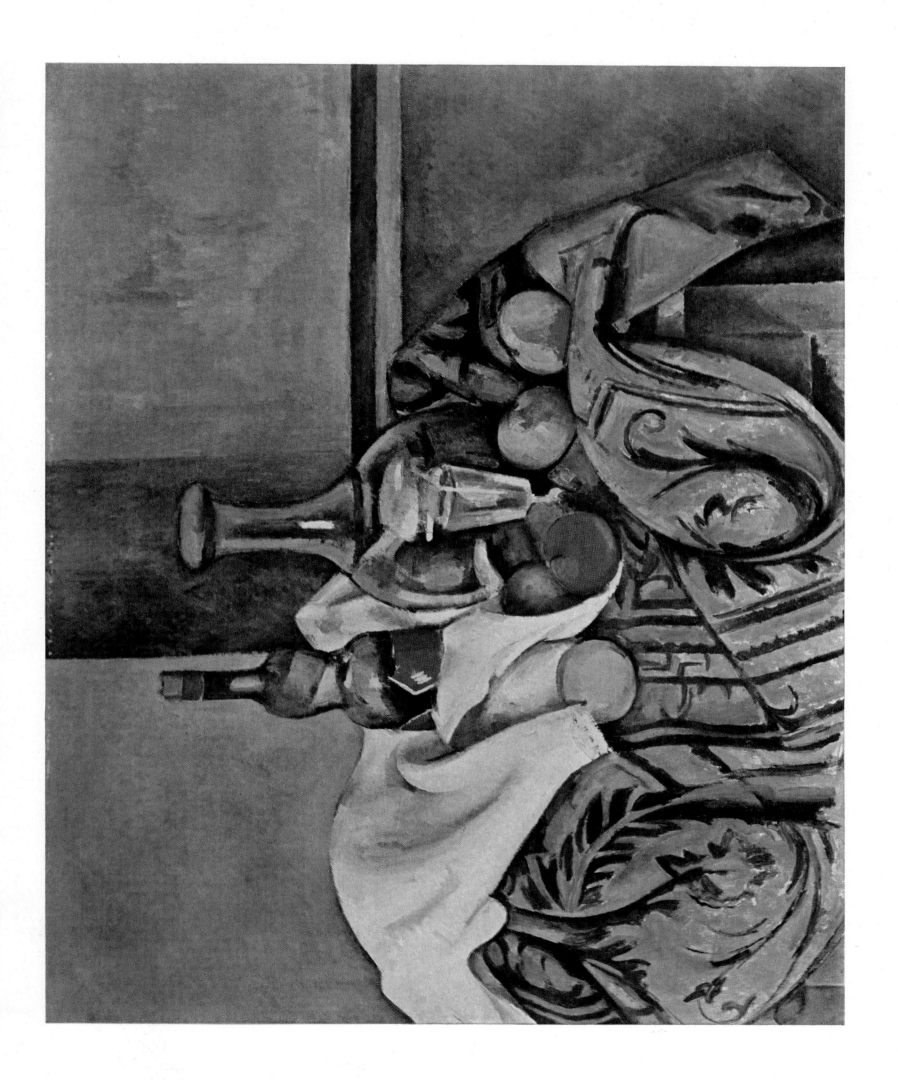